Under My Skin

CLAUDIA BUCKLEY

Copyright © 2021 Claudia Buckley

All rights reserved.

ISBN: 978-1-7776641-0-7

DEDICATION

To my family – immediate and extended – your patience, cooperation and understanding made this book possible. Your curiosity and enthusiasm made it worthwhile.

CONTENTS

	Preface	viii
Part 1	Walk With Me	1
	My Journey	2
	My Parents' Parents	18
	Soldiers, Saddlers & Scotsmen	75
Part 2	Reflections	94
Part 3	The Map	110
	References	133
	Appendix I – Cousins, Explained	136
	Appendix II – My Family Trees	137
	Appendix III – Resources Cheat Sheet	148
	A Word From the Author	151

ACKNOWLEDGMENTS

I must acknowledge that this entire project was a community effort. I received assistance from virtually everyone I came in contact with over the four-year span of my research – from family members who had a keen interest in seeing the results, to co-workers and strangers who patiently answered my requests for help in one way or another.

I make special mention of my parents, Claude and Joy, my Aunts Nerissa (Jean), Ava (Cathy) and Grandaunt Inez for understanding the vision and for sharing not just the stories but what also they meant to you and your loved ones then, and what they mean to you now. This book is yours in every sense of the word.

A great big thank you to my siblings who helped to jog some of my earliest memories. Kerry, Carolin, Suzie, Kirk, Junior and Ben – you guys are the best!

I am grateful to my copy editor Marsha Gray-Malcolm for taking this baby of mine from its embryotic stage to birth by providing me with guidance and tips to ensure a high-quality product.

I reserve my final expression of gratitude to my beautiful daughter Laurel and my supportive husband Mervyn. You have both come into my life and made me a better person than I was before. I am indebted to you for your unwavering motivation and honest feedback.

I have the best cheerleaders I could have ever asked for.

Preface

ARE YOU IN THE RIGHT PLACE?

DON'T read this book:

- if you have no interest in family stories, or in genealogy;
- if you're only interested in knowing the origin elements of your DNA, for example: 25% South Asian, or 16% European etc. I do talk about that a bit, but I don't go into too much detail about it, because my focus is on knowing actual family stories, and the ethnicity percentages are not yet an exact science anyway; or
- if you are a professional genealogist who already uncovers family history for yourself and others. If so, you likely will not benefit much from the tips in this book as it is mostly geared toward newer researchers looking for suggestions and tips.

DEFINITELY read this book:

- if you want to gather and organize your family history but have limited financial resources;
- if you want to put your family tree together but don't know where to start;

- if you want to know more about the lives of your grandparents or those before them;
- if you want to read how a complete amateur successfully pieced together over 200 years (and counting!) of the lives hundreds of family members and their stories using minimal resources, and
- if you want some inspiration to start your own digging.

This book is meant to be a starting point for those who, like me, thought it would be too much to expect to know anything definite about the different origins that run under their skin; those who went along with whatever we guessed from the shade of our skin, the shape of our lips or the texture of our hair. We were told that everything beyond that was lost. It's meant for the ones who sat in rueful silence when others spoke freely about their known ancestors from the 17th or 18th century who were busy forging a future for their descendants while ours were, essentially, faceless and unknown.

If you want to discover what you can learn from the lessons of generations of your family; if you want to listen to the stories told by the lives of your ancestors without breaking the bank, you are in the right place. Read on.

HOW TO USE THIS BOOK

This book basically has three major sections, as outlined below.

Part 1 – WALK WITH ME (My Journey)

This section serves a two-fold purpose. First of all, it narrates my own journey as I navigated through unfamiliar territory and made my own mistakes. Secondly, it documents and helps me to preserve the memories, stories and lessons of the deceased ancestors whom I sought and discovered. These are my actual and authentic family narratives, grouped by last names, hopefully inspiring you to understand what you can find with some patience and a bit of guidance.

Part 2 – REFLECTIONS (Lessons Learned)

Though I do interject little lessons I learned while telling each story in Part 1, in Part 2 I specifically share how this project has changed my overall thinking and opinions on important subjects. I compare the lives of my forebears with people I see every day, and sometimes with my own to see how much (and whether) things have actually changed.

Part 3 – THE MAP (Your Journey)

Part 3 is a seven-step blueprint for how to start your own journey, and how to know when you are finished. Importantly, it also tells you what to do when you are in the middle and stuck. I will share my own tips and those of experts, which will hopefully help you to avoid some of the mistakes I made, so you don't waste time re-inventing the wheel. I have also included a *Cheat Sheet* (Appendix III) of websites, books and other resources that I found useful and which will no doubt benefit you too.

Feel free to read the book in any order, but in my opinion, reading sections in the order in which they appear would be more helpful to a beginner.

PART 1
WALK WITH ME

My Journey

The "Why?"

In a scene from the 1997 historical drama, Amistad, director Stephen Spielberg depicts a conversation between the sixth President of the United States and fictional character Theodore Joadson. Adams asks Joadson what was "the story" of the Africans who were at the center of the movie's plot. In the film, Adams explained that a person's "story" wasn't just about where they were born, but was more about what got them to where they were now.

I watched Amistad in January 2017. The scene above was not the most memorable to me, but I do recall that immediately after watching the movie, I asked myself what was my story. I had been especially motivated by my teenaged daughter, who had been pressing me for years to look up and to document our family tree using the frequently-advertised websites which offer the service. She readily admits now that she is easily influenced by heavy advertising, and she's right. Ancestry.com reeled her in pretty well and convinced her impressionable young mind that this would be a worthwhile investment. My response for as long as I can remember was, "That's not for our people. Our history is so mixed up it can't be traced."

To a certain extent, it seemed that Ancestry

agreed with me too. At that time, the commercials which were shown on TV all depicted Caucasian Americans who were able to find "hints" to connect them to their great grandfather who was a war hero, or their grandaunt who married the inventor of some 19th century technology. At that time, I never saw any commercials which showed people of color who found family records, or got hints added to their family trees by clicking on names.

As far as I was concerned, I could go back as far as my oldest living relative could remember and then that would be it – our detailed distant history was not preserved anywhere, and knowing where you are from was the privilege of the colonizers. I figured I would encounter the proverbial "brick wall" long before getting to know any of my ancestors who had been enslaved. The fact is, I had never really heard my parents speaking in any kind of detail about anyone earlier than their grandparents, who, in both cases, had raised them.

To further complicate matters, I am from the island of Jamaica, and Jamaican families are almost always a web of half-siblings, unknown parents, "pet" names, informally adopted and "jacket" children (which is the colorful term used to describe a child whose alleged father is not, in fact, the biological father. The idea is that of a garment which can be easily thrown onto a person and can blend with the outfit even if the jacket isn't the wearer's perfect fit. That's where I think the term originated, anyway).

One DNA consulting company in Jamaica revealed that in 70% of their tests, the men who were named as fathers had nothing to do with the paternity of the children named. Now, this doesn't mean that 70% of all Jamaican men are wearing "jackets" (the fact that they went to get the DNA test in the first place says that there may have already been an element of doubt). A 2019 study conducted by an anthropologist at the University of the West Indies suggests that the figure is closer to 25%. That's still uncomfortably high. With those kinds of numbers in mind, you can imagine how difficult, discouraging and frustrating this kind of search would be for the average Jamaican.

In spite of this, after many years my daughter wore me down. In about 2017, I decided to appease her. I would do her family tree by talking to my relatives and her dad's relatives. I would locate a few stories and share them with her. I wanted it to be as expansive as was practical, to include aunts, uncles and cousins, but I expected it would go back three generations and take two to three weeks, maximum. Boy, was I wrong!

The Journey Begins

I love a good challenge. Couple that with these new missions and I felt like I was filling someone's need for information, albeit one created by my own announcement. So I dived right in, starting from next to zero with this brief family history, my laptop and internet connection as my only tools.

My very first scribble was about a relative who had migrated to Panama in the early 1900s. My mother said her name was Celena Thompson, and that she was related in some way to Mabel Ambursley (later Drummond), my mom's paternal grandmother. There was a family story that Celena had gone to Panama with the title for some family land and she never came back to Jamaica. And that was all she knew. I just jotted:

"Celena Thompson (Panama) relative of Mabel Drummond"

I realized pretty early on that scribbling info like this on bits of paper or even in a book without a system in place was a really bad idea. I would go back a day or two later and find it hard to remember or understand what all the little connecting lines meant, or I realized that I couldn't read some of the inserts I added when I updated my info. It also wasn't practical for me to use an online resource as my everyday organizer, because I was getting all kinds of info from the internet and my relatives – names, dates, anecdotes I never asked for but which would probably be useful later, occupations, locations etc. I needed to put all this random information in a place that put some structure to the randomness, which I could easily access and use later. So I made my own personalized journal and got myself organized. For tips on how you can do this, take a look at Part 3, Tip 3 ("Getting It All Organized").

Back to Celena Thompson. I think I wanted to be the hero who tracked down the documents which had been missing for 100 years. To be fair, I didn't really think how it would play out. What would the "answer" look like, and would I know it if I saw it? I had absolutely no idea, but I was excited!

I went to Google and typed her name in. Naturally, nothing significant appeared. But I stumbled upon a website that appeared to be (and was!) completely free. It allowed me to type in the name of a deceased person and by providing some parameters to create filters, I could browse actual documents like birth and death certificates, census and sailing records and the like.

The short version is that with this excellent open-source data available online, I found a document which was an application for a "Photo-Metal Check" by a janitress of the QMD in the Panama Canal. I had to research what a "Photo-Metal Check" was. The US Government's archives catalog states the intent of establishing a Photo-Metal Check system in the Panama Canal Zone was to positively identify individuals and to allow their entry into restricted areas, similar to the system used by munitions plants and navy yards in the United States. Once approved by the Executive Office, the official photographer would then schedule office units or work gangs to have their photographs taken at the official photographic studio in either Balboa or Cristobal. It was a sort of application for what we would call security clearance, or a background check, to get a work permit today.

With the information from my mom, I typed in Celena's name, place of birth and approximate year of birth among the available Panama records. I got about six hits, but one in particular stood out. This particular applicant was C. Thompson from Westmoreland, Jamaica. Her picture, monthly wage, date of birth and physical features were recorded on the application. I sent a picture of the document to my mom's phone with the caption, "Could this be Celena Thompson?"

The response, "99.5% it is Celena," sent me whoop-whooping and almost had me clicking my heels. A relative of mine, from 100 years ago, had left some trace of herself on the worldwide web! It said that she was born on July 26, 1896 and she arrived on the Panamanian isthmus on November 13, 1911. Assuming that the given dates were correct, that would have made her 15 years old when she arrived. I frowned when I saw that, because it seemed unlikely that Celena would have migrated to begin working at that young age. I looked back at the other five records that appeared with hers. Apparently, it was by no means uncommon. Several other documents I found likewise showed young men, aged 15 and even 14 years old.

The call for workers was advertised in The Daily Gleaner newspaper. Most ordinary people were small-time farmers, peasants, barely surviving off their own land, or working on large coffee, banana or sugar cane plantations for wealthy landowners. Most saw the existing situation as a new name for an old situation – being tied to a circumstance which they would not overcome in their lifetime without some drastic change. Naturally, the desire to leave plantation life was very strong. As long as the land was owned by the same folks who had made slavery legal, the idea of emancipation only existed on paper.

So as soon as the opportunity presented itself, Afro-Jamaicans realized that the best way to truly 'free' themselves from the cycle of working on someone else's land was to purchase the land themselves. The general intention was to accept work on an intense working-blitz overseas, and return home with enough money to buy land and a new way of life. This happened throughout Jamaican history, and basically, is still happening today.

Celena apparently sent money back home, as many did, but never went back to Jamaica herself. I was not able to find any more documents to figure out what became of her in Panama, or indeed, if she moved on as some did, along the Central American coast to Nicaragua, Belize or Costa Rica for other opportunities. What we do know, and what my mother tried to impress upon us was the great sacrifice she made so that our family could own the land where my great grandmother, grandfather and mother lived, and which we as kids took for granted while growing up. My grandfather and granduncle are buried there, and my Auntie Hopie lives there now.

Having read as much as I have about the working conditions of Caribbean workers in the Panama Canal Zone, I now completely understand why my mom speaks so passionately about Celena and why she wants to ensure that that little piece of land in Grange Hill, Westmoreland stays in the family. Workers would send whatever money they made to invest in property, or to help support family members who were left back home. Men lost their limbs and lives doing dangerous work for which neither they nor their families received any compensation.

Afro-Caribbean workers faced outright racism and were restricted from traveling to certain sections of the country. In 1928 the constitution declared that their children, despite being born and raised in Panama, were denied citizenship until at least their 21st birthday, at which point these children had to satisfy several legal requirements, including proof that they had received all their education in Panama and that Spanish was the language spoken at home. In 1941, approximately 20,000 Panamanians of West Indian descent who had been born after 1928 were effectively denationalized when an even more aggressive legislation barred them from naturalization altogether. Anti-West Indian sentiments seemed to be getting worse until 1945 when a new constitution was formed, reversing the exclusionist laws and allowing equal citizenship rights to all members of the Panamanian community.

Since finding Celena, I've spent many nights searching, researching, scribbling and scratching for the stories behind the names.

What Are You Looking for?

My maternal grand-aunts and others of their generation talk about "Old Boothe" like he was a god. There is a picture of him — a shrine, really — in a little corner of their living rooms, and they can really keep you locked down for quite some time if you make the mistake of asking, "Who's that?" So the first summer after I moved to Canada, I took my then-preteen daughter to visit her great-grandaunt and naturally she fell into the trap. She asked who "Old Boothe" was and just got stories and references to other characters whom I really didn't really know either, or only had a vague idea of who they were. They were just names that I had always heard thrown about, and I never imagined that today I would be scrambling to find out more about them before the closest sources of information leave us.

Throughout my research, I often found myself having to redefine the true purpose of my study. Why was I spending so much time on this project? What was my end game? What questions was I trying to answer and what was I hoping to accomplish? I often found myself going down rabbit hole after rabbit hole, getting sidetracked, being frustrated, annoying co-workers, family members and other acquaintances with what seemed to be a pointless exercise in looking up "dead people".

I admit that there were long stretches where I stopped working on this project altogether, because I felt it was consuming my time with no tangible benefit to anyone alive. But there was one person whose curiosity never wavered – my daughter's. Any mention I made of an old relative was met with genuine interest and questions which I had either thought of myself, or to which I was now interested in getting the answers. I think what I learned from this is that there is a natural childish curiosity and fascination we all have about people, places and stories but which we seem to lose as we grow older. We get bogged down with our jobs, making a living and surviving in this world every day because we just don't have the time, or don't see the practicality in getting the answers to these questions. The questions resurface when our lives slow down a bit, or when our own children ask them. By then, we are running out of time because the holders of the family histories are leaving us, and the stories are getting lost.

So, no matter how often I set this project aside, I always found myself coming back to it. There was always that lingering obligation to finish what I had started for fear of regretting it. I also figured that every single member of my family had a natural curiosity about the stories of their family members, even if our motivations are different, and that one day they would be happy that someone took the time to record them.

Now, think about this: going back only three generations, you would have 14 direct ancestors (seven men and seven women). Each of these likely had children other than your parents and grandparents. So there are aunts, uncles and a host of cousins, all of whom had their own lives and stories begging to be shared. Many of these were very tempting, and it is easy to reason, "Surely, these are members of my family too. Why shouldn't their stories be told?" But I soon came to see the folly of this type of reasoning. As my mother always says, "Everybody has a story." I really had to define my purpose, and not get sidetracked by the other stories I was bound to stumble upon. It would be impossible to complete what I set out to do if I attempted to tell everyone's story in this particular project.

With this reminder, at some point I decided that I had to define my objectives by taking the time to document what exactly it was that I wanted to find. What questions did I want answered? There were so many! And even more got asked along the way. But I could only stay focused if I actually put those questions down in writing. Here were the questions I started with:

- I was fascinated by my maternal relatives, the ones from Westmoreland, who, as far as I know, farmed land as long as anyone could remember and owned significant parcels of land in that area as well as St. Elizabeth. How did that come about? How did they go about owning these lands when all indications were that they had been common labourers who descended from enslaved Africans? My mother's surname at birth, Fairclough, was fairly uncommon. She speculated that we were related to Osmond Theodore (O.T.) Fairclough, co-founder of one of the two major political parties in Jamaica. Was that true? I wanted all the stories!

- Was I really Irish on my father's side? How, if at all, was I related to national hero Alexander Bustamante as had been claimed over and over by my father and repeated by us within the family?
- What was the mystery behind my husband's paternal family? My husband had discovered in adulthood that he had older half-siblings on his dad's side. We knew nothing about them. Why not? Neither did we know his grandparents. Who were they and what was their story?
- Could I dare expect to find out the composition of my ancestry? Jamaica has chosen the national and cultural motto: "Out of many, one people"; who were my "many", my "people"? Where did my ancestors hail from, and how far could I go? What and who were really beneath my skin?

What I found really interesting was that my

questions changed. My relationship to well-known people became less and less important when I saw how the ordinary, everyday people contributed far more to the values my family and I hold dear. Through hard work and despite difficult circumstances, they made tough decisions and took risks. Some turned out well, and some didn't, but their bravery was no less than that of celebrated political figures or others with obvious advantages.

Bustamante and O.T. Fairclough had enough relatives claiming kinship. My overworked, unpaid and uneducated ancestors needed someone to talk about their stories, so in time I redirected my research and rose to that challenge.

You may find yourself in that position too. You may uncover a family secret and find that the "characters" start pulling you in another direction to tell their story. When that happens, it's a beautiful thing; just embrace it.

I have always been interested in societies – how they behave and why they change. I believe a good insight on the peculiarities of any society would come from understanding how that society worked in the past, how its people lived and how those factors shaped the present. So I guess I was also indirectly doing some sociological research, relating what life might have been like for the pre- and post-emancipation generations by documenting the experiences of my own relatives who lived during that period, and how our family has evolved since then.

DNA Evidence

In December 2017 I decided to kick this project up a notch by taking up the offer of the various advertisers to find out who "my people" really were – with a DNA test. After mulling over it for months, I ordered a kit and spent the next four weeks waiting with great anticipation.

I knew what I was expecting – predominantly West African with a bit of European (I expected Irish because that is what my dad told us). I predicted a 75:25 or so ratio, even though I had started having my doubts, since in all my research I could not find any concrete evidence of any European ancestors whatsoever.

Around mid-January 2018, the email notifying me of my results came in. I could barely contain my excitement! I was going to find out my origins! I quickly located the relevant report and scrolled down to the "Ancestry Composition" chart. The testing company estimated that I was about a 99% African/European mix, with the remaining 1% being possibly Native American and/or other unidentified origins. The report gave a further breakdown showing specific regions in West Africa as well as Northwestern and Southern Europe where my ancestors would have called home. From what they could identify, about 11.5% was attributed to European ancestry of some sort, so 87.5% was African.

Well, that was a surprise! The ostracism I had

dealt with for most of my primary school years was all for nothing but the actual shade of my skin.

The membrane that covers my internal organs has a yellowish undertone, sort of a latte, or golden tan complexion. At least that's what the makeup I buy tells me the color is. I have vivid memories of being teased as a "malatta" (mulatto) while I was in the second grade. It was made worse by the fact that I had been transferred to that class about two months after the start of the school year, so I already stood out like a sore thumb. I was jeered, scorned and physically bullied. Up until that early transfer to the second grade, I had no idea that I looked any different from anyone else. Somehow, being called various names, including "dundus" (albino) all those years ago must have convinced me that I was "other" than my classmates and the average Jamaican I bumped into daily.

However, now, 30-something years later, I was being told that I was no different from them. In fact, I probably had more African DNA than some of my assailants. It was estimated that I have predominantly Nigerian ancestry, and there are known African peoples with very pale skin, including the Igbos, the Khoi, the Ewes and others. Now, I understand that DNA testing companies cannot claim absolute accuracy in pinpointing locations, but scientists generally agree that ancestry estimates are broadly correct up to around eight generations back. That would be about 250 years ago. This was what I had meant when I had told daughter about never being absolutely certain about the full story of my ancestors – where they definitely came from and how they got here, but at least putting some context to it all was better than nothing. And having gotten started, I wasn't about to give up at that point.

My Parents' Parents

Fairclough (or, as my Mom would say, "Fair-clo")

It seemed like the Fairclough branch of my family tree would be a good starting point. It wasn't a common name, so I reasoned that anyone with that name would be an obvious relative. Fairclough was my mother's name before marriage. We grew up hearing her pronounce it to rhyme with "dough". I would occasionally hear people say "Faircluff" (to rhyme with "rough"), but my mom would instantly and firmly rebuff them, saying, "My name is pronounced 'Fairclo'!" I would chime in and correct them too, thinking at first that they didn't know how to pronounce it properly, and later, that it was an alternate pronunciation that I needed to educate them on. When I became an adult, I realized that absolutely no one else in Jamaica with that name said 'Fairclo'. I don't know why she (still) insists on this pronunciation, but I've concluded that "Faircloff" (to rhyme with "cough") is probably the pronunciation closest to the original Old English pronunciation and meaning, 'a fair (or beautiful) clough, cliff or ravine'. It's also my compromise between saying "cluff", which my mom hates, and saying the unpopular and strange-sounding "clo".

Anyway, I say all of the above in order to

explain that I started with the Faircloughs as they were my closest known relatives with an unusual name which should have been fairly simple to piece together. Add that to the fact that I had gone to school in Westmoreland (where my mother was from) for two years, met my husband there and lived there for a while after we got married. I had also been fairly close to my grandfather (Papa) before he died, and my maternal siblings and I considered Grange Hill, Westmoreland to be our "country" because we would spend so much time there. So Westmoreland was really home. I was familiar with the geography, and I still have connections to the area by way of family land.

I was a little surprised when I realized that my mother knew the name of her grandfather and not much more. Her father, Oswald, was raised by his mother Mabel Ambursley but not his father, Caleb Fairclough.

I cannot express the frustration I felt when I could find no record of either Papa or his father in the public archives. It was as if neither of them had existed! I did, however, find Papa's brother Norman, who had died tragically when he was only six years old. His death was clearly documented. My granduncle Norman Fairclough's death certificate reads, "Misadventure having been struck by a motorcar driven by Edmund James. No one criminally responsible for his death. Inquest held 6th January 1931." The story, as told by my mother, goes something like this.

My grandfather Oswald was two years younger than his brother Norman, and as children they would walk home from school together. They would take a shortcut through a neighbour's yard which was just up the street. But one Thursday in December of 1930 was the last day that happened. My mom says the two boys were holding hands and walking through the usual path when a dog chased them off their course. They ran out into the road and were hit by a passing car. Frightened neighbours rushed to tell Miss Mabel that her two boys had been killed. As it turned out, only one boy had actually died, but the other one, who later became my grandfather, was so badly hurt that they didn't expect him to live. But he did survive. It took him the better part of a year to get back to normal as he had to learn to walk all over again and, as my Auntie Jean tells it, he became his mother's favourite as a result of the tragedy.

While searching for Papa's name, I found an article about the accident in the Daily Gleaner newspaper of January 10, 1931. I couldn't believe my eyes! This was more than I ever expected. I found this article about the death of my young granduncle in February 2018, about a year after I started my research. The headline was "SCHOOLBOY IS KILLED ON ROAD BY MOTORCAR" with subheadings:

"Jury Finds That No One Is Responsible For Death of Norman Fairclough",

"RAN ACROSS THE ROAD"

"Two Children Dashed Out From Track Only A Few Feet In Front Of Car."

That sort of summed everything up for anyone who didn't want to read the lengthy article. But I did want to read it, of course. It was the coroner's inquest, and it included the witness statements verbatim, as well as the statement of Mabel Ambursley, the mother of the two boys, my own great-grandmother. My mother hadn't even known of the existence of the article until I found and shared it with her. I sat with her and read it aloud. She was quiet, reflective, sad. She thought about her grandmother who received no compensation, monetary or otherwise, for the death of one son and the injury of the other. Maybe my aunt was right. Maybe that is why Mabel was so protective of the surviving son and maybe she did give him preferential treatment growing up.

Now I was interested in the stories of the characters involved in the incident. I was curious about the driver of the car. Where was he going and what was his state of mind? What did onlookers have to say?

The driver of the car, Edmund Haughton James, testified that he was driving from Grange Hill toward the town of Savanna-la-mar at about 20 miles per hour when he saw two children run out from a track. The children were six or seven feet away from his car when he saw them. He swerved to the right and pressed his brakes, but the accident could not be avoided and the children were struck.

Testimony also came from travelling salesman Wills O'Gilvie Isaacs, who was the passenger in the offending Dodge motorcar. Isaacs said more or less the same thing: 20 miles per hour, children five to seven feet away, brakes applied, accident unavoidable. Aubrey Jones, sworn in as an eyewitness: same.

I was skeptical. It seemed unlikely to me that a car going that slowly made such an impact that the child was killed on the spot. I was also suspicious that people who were going about their own business would have been paying attention to a car going at 20 miles per hour when, from all indications, this was a normal day. But my mother said that since motor vehicles were rather uncommon in those days, people were probably paying attention whenever one came along.

The eyewitness to the car accident, Aubrey Jones, was the manager at the local Public Works Station.

What put the icing on the cake for me though, was that after all the testimonies had been heard, the magistrate addressed the jury by pointing out that his own personal opinion was that the accident could not have been avoided and THEN asked them for their verdict. Naturally, James was found not guilty by the ten men of the jury, including one Sadler Haughton James (by some stroke of coincidence he shared the same uncommon last name as the defendant)!

The Haughton-James family was for all intents

and purposes fairly well-known in Westmoreland. The earliest record of this family was in the early 1700s, where John Haughton-James Jr. was the executor of Kings Valley estate, a mere two miles away from where my family lived in Lincoln, Grange Hill.

I say all of this to say this driver was fortunate that his boss knew some pretty well-connected and influential community members in a town where neither of them lived nor was raised. My great grandmother, who could barely read and write and who wasn't at the scene of the accident when it happened, could not refute the ridiculous defense. Furthermore, the very coroner who from all indications should have been serving as impartial judge, had already told the jury his opinion so the case was pretty much closed.

To be fair, I'm not sure that sending anyone to prison under these circumstances would have accomplished much. Obviously, there was no malicious intent that caused the accident. It was truly that – an accident – and no matter what a judge decided, it wouldn't have brought Norman back.

I just can't help but reflect on how dynamic this thing called life is. My mother and her siblings never met their uncle Norman. We don't know who he would have been or what he would have done. So how did these men who were unintentionally involved in his death fare later? My hours of research revealed some really interesting facts about the direction their lives took.

To begin with, the driver was a chauffeur by profession who was from Kingston. This got me curious. He must have been driving someone of considerable status in those days for that person to have a personal driver. So who was this passenger? He was the previously-mentioned salesman, Wills O'Gilvie Isaacs. Make that the Wills O'Gilvie Isaacs, later to become a very prominent politician and Jamaica's High Commissioner to Canada. Isaacs' own son, William, was born just three weeks after the accident (December 27), but on December 16 the following year, almost one year to the day after my granduncle's death, William's mother died. She was only 30 years old. Mr. Isaacs remarried the daughter of a Westmoreland businessman and Justice of the Peace in 1942, and then married again in 1950. He eventually retired from politics and died in 1981.

His son William later entered politics and was a prominent member of Prime Minister Michael Manley's cabinet in the 1970s.

But I digress. Where was my grandfather Oswald Fairclough in the records? After many weeks of putting the Fairclough search aside, one day out of the blue and when I wasn't searching for it at all, I stumbled across the record of an "Aswald Anthony Ambursley." What?! I blinked. It was still there. Sure enough, his mother was Mabel Ambursley, and he was born in Grange Hill, Westmoreland in 1926. But how could this be? Why was he registered as Ambursley, and why had none of us known this before? Well, my great-grandmother never married Caleb Fairclough. It occurred to me not long after, that this could be the reason that, when my aunt went to report Papa's death in 2010, the records office was unable to find his record of birth. Of course, she was looking for Oswald Fairclough, but he was actually registered under his mother's surname.

The process of registering the birth of a child at that time usually involved informing the postmistress of the desired name. For the majority of under-educated Jamaicans, this meant that the postmistress often went with a phonetic spelling of the Jamaican pronunciation of the name given. "Oswald" probably sounded more like "Aswald" in Mabel's Westmoreland accent, and so my grandfather was registered as "Aswald". And none of us knew his true registered name until eight years after his death. Mystery solved.

Armed with that nugget of information, I resumed my search, this time focusing on my granduncle Lebert, known to us as "Uncle Bredda", using the last name "Ambursley." Looking back, it never seemed strange to us as children that we were essentially calling him "Uncle Brother". It's funny now, but it seemed perfectly normal to us then. Kind of like how my mom is known to everyone with whom she grew up as "Sister". The explanation is that she was her mother's third child, the first two being my Aunt Jean and my

Uncle Trevor. So, when the new baby (my mother) was born, she became the sister! Her permanent name to all in the community was (and still is) "Sister".

I remember the first time I heard about that. I may have been about nine years old. It was new and unusual for me to think of my mother as a child, and especially as the little sister. I thought of my own little brothers, five and seven years younger than I was, and how I viewed them when they were newborns. They needed my protection and my care as an older sister. I babied them and fussed over them like they were the most precious babies in the world. My mother was that same infant to my aunt and uncle. She bore the title Little Sister. Up until that point, her only titles to me had been All-Knowing, All-Wise Mother; Teacher-of-Facts; Fixer-of-Problems; Disciplinarian. But to her siblings she was a sibling, and the baby one at that!

I think my daughter went through the same epiphany when I overheard a conversation between her and my sister's daughter. The girls are only three months apart, and they were about six or seven years old at the time. My niece was informing Laurel, "My mom is older than your mom. That means she can whoop your mom." I stifled my laughter from my unseen hiding place. My daughter was visibly upset and disappointed. She had to settle for being the younger cousin, and to add insult to injury, she also had to settle for her mom being the younger sister. She made some comment to the effect of it being "unfair" and stormed away. My niece was actually quite right. My sister is nine years older than I am, not the mere three- and six-year age difference between my mother and her older siblings. My sister could (and probably still can) whoop me quite soundly.

Anyway, back to Uncle Bredda. I searched for Lebert Fairclough, Lebert Ambursely, Ambursly and Ambersley. Many, many, many hours later, I found him, not as Lebert, but as "Nebest Emanuel Ambursley". This is not as far-fetched as you might initially imagine. The handwritten document actually looked like it said "Nebert", with that type of cursive "r" which could have easily been an "r", an "s" or even an "n", and so when the document was converted to a digital format for us inquiring minds, the transcriber recorded it as "Nebest". That "N" though, could hardly be anything but an "N". Was my granduncle really "Nebert" all these years and for some reason, it was Lebert that stuck? This is the kind of detective work that I dealt with for the better part of three years.

I couldn't find any records for Caleb Fairclough, my grandfather's dad. However, I did find a 1919 death certificate for Mabel's two-year-old son, Hubert Fairclough. Their place of residence at the time was Chester Castle, Hanover. All the evidence suggests that this was Caleb's son. All their subsequent children were born in Grange Hill, Westmoreland, where Mabel had been raised.

Caleb also had an older daughter, Eva, by

another woman. My mom confirmed knowing this aunt of hers, and I found Eva's birth certificate, documenting her place of birth as Chester Castle. Aunt Eva died in 2009 in Maldon, St. James. There is a group of Faircloughs in rural St. James to whom I believe I am related through this same Caleb Fairclough.

This link to Chester Castle, which borders the parishes of Westmoreland, Hanover and St. James, is why I believe my mother is convinced of our connection to Osmond ("O.T.") Fairclough, co-founder of one of the two major political parties in Jamaica. O.T.'s grandfather, Edward Morris Fairclough, raised his family in Bethel Town, Westmoreland and nearby Montpelier, St. James. I never dug deep enough to find out whether there was, in fact, a link between the two families. I realized that proving or disproving my familial ties to

well-known people didn't add any value to me personally; I was far more interested in the lives of those close to me, and how their stories set the stage for my own life.

Here is a curious story that I still haven't gotten to the bottom of, but I fully intend to do so someday. Here in Canada, I have a good friend to whom I casually mentioned that I was doing family research. I must have mentioned the name Fairclough, because he lightly chuckled, "Maybe we are cousins; my family is Fairclough too."

My eyes narrowed. "Are you serious?" I asked.
"Yeah."

My husband jumped on it. "Wait a minute, Claudia! He looks just like your uncle!"

He was right. My mom's brother, who is the spitting image of Papa Fairclough, was practically looking back at me in my friend's face. How had I never noticed this before? I quickly reached for my cellphone and retrieved my uncle's Facebook page. I showed his picture to my friend and his wife.

"Whoa," My friend sat down. "This man is my family," he admitted.

My friend disclosed that his maternal grandmother was Fairclough, but that he was not very familiar with that side of his family. That seems to be the history of so many Jamaicans. I don't know why. So many people have no relationship with an entire side of the family. I mean, I watch enough television to know that this is not a situation unique to Jamaica, but I think I am now slowly realizing that the proportion in my homeland is probably higher than in most other places. Growing up, I heard the explanation that the lack of permanent family ties due to acts of slave-trading has led to a casual view of family ties, especially paternal responsibilities. I do not know enough about family relationships in other Caribbean territories to confirm or refute this theory, but knowing what I now know, I am inclined to admit that this may indeed be true. Sad, and true.

But back to my mom's grandmother, Mabel Ambursley, and her children. Doing the Ambursley search, I also found three more of Papa's siblings whom I had never heard of before. Hubert, who lived only two years, died in 1919. Then almost ten years later, Josephine died in 1928 at 15 months old, and Isett (or Ivett), just three weeks shy of her first birthday, died in the same year as my granduncle Norman, in 1930. So just like that, my great-grandmother's brood of six little ones became two. To bury one child is heartbreaking. To bury four children in the space of eleven years is unimaginable. I mentioned Hubert, Josephine and Ivett to my mother. She had not been aware of their existence.

Our relatives in the early 20th century must have led some very sad lives. I found out that it was the exception to have all one's children survive to adulthood. Parent after parent went through the trauma of burying their children. I'm not sure how this affected them psychologically, but perhaps that's why they had so many children – not knowing who would succumb to something as simple as a fever, a cold or a cough because of not having ready access to reliable medical attention – this was their way of ensuring that they didn't end up childless, I suppose.

All my life, I had only known of the two siblings, my grandfather Oswald and his brother Lebert. They lived next door to each other on the same plot of land where they were raised in

Sterling, Grange Hill, Westmoreland. And they never... ever... spoke to each other. I'm serious. My siblings and I never saw my grandfather and granduncle exchange a word. They both died when I was a little over 30 years old and not once in 30 years had I seen them speak to each other. When we asked the reason for that, my mother would vaguely say, "Oh, some disagreement they had as boys." And that was that. Never anything more than that. The explanation never changed or expanded in any way. What I do remember though, is that whenever we went to visit Papa, he would always ask, "Did you go and look for your uncle?" (meaning my granduncle, of course). And he would make sure we went.

My mother doesn't know what caused this, and neither does my Auntie Jean. Not for sure, anyway. Auntie Jean says it was jealousy that Papa was their mother's favourite. She says my great-grandmother Mabel had acquired a soft spot for him after the accident and that she had spoiled him ever since, but it doesn't seem likely to me that you would stop speaking with your only sibling because of that. Not for over 50 years! I'm pretty sure it was something more specific than that. Who knows, maybe even they didn't remember what their disagreement had been about. Or maybe they did, and they had long forgiven each other but each was too proud to be the first to make a move. Whatever the story, I guess we will never know now. Uncle Bredda died in 2003 and Papa in 2010.

Oswald "Papa" Fairclough in his later years – always in good spirits

After the series of tragedies in the early 1930s, Mabel married Walter Drummond in 1938. Again, Mabel soon had another funeral to plan. Walter didn't live very long. I don't know the date of his death, but my mother said she only knew that he died a few years after he and Mabel got married. My mom herself never knew him, and she was born in the 1950's. Mabel died in 1972, and my mother moved to Montego Bay that same year in search of work in the city. She made Montego Bay her home and that is where she met my father.

Old Boothe & Other "Famous" Relatives

As mentioned before, a somewhat distant relative of mine who was known as Old Boothe should probably be credited with being one of the sources of my initial fascination. My mother's aunts revere him, speaking in glowing terms as if he were second only to the Messiah. At the last family gathering I remember them talking about him as usual, but since asking who he actually was or what he did to deserve such attention would have been like asking who Michael Jackson was, I stayed quiet. But based on what I could gather from the conversation, he was my grandmother's well-to-do grandfather who had owned the property which I heard was our original family land, in Brighton, Westmoreland. I heard glowing stories of a mansion situated on a sprawling hillside. Whenever we were driving through nearby Bluefields as a child, the hillside was often pointed out to us. "All that land belongs to the family, you know," my mom would say.

But with all the history I had begun to uncover, I realized that Old Boothe would have come from humble beginnings. I simply had to find out how all this land came into our possession.

By far, most of the DNA cousins I have found online are related to me by my Boothe relatives. The main reason, of course, is that they were for the most part, prolific reproducers. My mother's mom was one of six siblings; her mother Eleanor Boothe was one of eight, and Eleanor's father was one of 10. If each of those 24 people had only two kids, we are talking about 48 cousins of varying degrees, not even counting their kids. And, believe me, they didn't have only two kids each. So I've found hundreds of people related to me just through my grandmother's maternal grandparents alone.

My mom's mother Inez, known to everyone as "Rose"

"Old Boothe" was my grandmother's grandfather, Walter. He and his wife Agnes lived at a really important turning point in Jamaica's history. Their parents had been born just after the full abolition of enslavement practices in Jamaica, but it was Walter's generation that would be the first to venture out into the wider world of their own accord in pursuit of better prospects. In what had turned out to be a huge political and social experiment, Afro-Jamaicans who were "born free" were now navigating and exploring an entirely new space because they felt they could now do as the colonizers had done – go abroad to seek their own fortune.

The reality is that after forced/free labour was made completely illegal in 1838, the economy in Jamaica collapsed. Well, of course it would. If an entire economy had been propped up purely on an endless supply of unpaid workers and that supply suddenly came to an end, you can imagine the inconvenience that would bring to the beneficiaries of such a system. They were simply unprepared for a workforce which now had to be paid for their labour, and which now had the right to refuse to work. The business model had been unsustainable.

I won't get into the matter of some measures the landowners took to force "free" people into working for as close to nothing as possible, nor into the formulation of new words for the same old practice ("slavery/apprenticeship/indentured labour"): that's the subject of another book. What I do want to talk about is what my grandmother's grandparents, who were born into such a society, decided to do about it, and what it tells me about their decisions then and our decisions now.

A Trip to Costa Rica

Walter and Agnes were born in 1869 and 1873 respectively. They got married in 1895. Walter was a shopkeeper in the district of Belmont, Westmoreland, the eldest of his brothers and sisters. By this time, indentured workers from India, China, Africa and even Europe had been coming to Jamaica for the past 50 years to supplement the short supply of cheap labour. The new generation of which Walter was a part, by and large refused to work on the sugar cane plantations which carried such negative memories for their parents and grandparents.

The newlyweds lived close to Agnes' parents and wasted no time in starting a family. Baby Thomas came nine months after the wedding, then came Lester in 1898 and my grandmother's mom Eleanor in 1900. Daisy was born in Jamaica in 1904, but by 1905 Walter and Agnes showed up as parents of two children born in Costa Rica. One was Daniel and the other was a daughter who died shortly after birth. It seems that they were twins.

I was very surprised to learn about this period in their lives. No one in my family had ever spoken about Costa Rica. I had so many questions! Why Costa Rica?

I imagine that what brought this on was the fact that when slavery and apprenticeship officially went out the window in 1838, most of the landowners abandoned their fields and returned home to England or Scotland in order to claim compensation from the government for their expected loss of revenue. Jamaica's archival records document that by 1849, 140 sugar cane and 465 coffee plantations totaling over 350,000 acres had been completely abandoned.

Attempts to become self-sufficient by planting and trading at local markets within the newly-established villages were met with heavy taxation devised by the remaining plantation owners in a bid to entice workers back to the few properties which were still in operation. When this didn't work, the colonial governors went seeking other sources of free labour and in 1845, managed to secure indentured workers, mostly from India, for the next 72 years. This worry was conveyed to the British Governor in Mauritius:

The abolition of slavery has rendered the British Colonies the scene of an experiment whether the staple products of imperial countries can be raised as effectually and as advantageously by the labour of free men as by that of slaves. To bring that momentous question to a fair trial, it is requisite that no unnecessary discouragement should be given to the introduction of free labourers into our colonies.
- British Colonial Secretary. Edward Stanley to Mauritian Governor William Gomm, 22 January, 1842.

With wages being low, and a poor economic

outlook anyway, many Afro-Jamaicans chose to look elsewhere for opportunities.

It is an understatement to say that the Costa Rican government's project to build a railway for the transportation of their coffee crop from the interior, across the steaming jungle to the port, was ambitious. A big clue was that local Costa Ricans wanted nothing to do with the venture. What with malaria, yellow fever and the poisonous snakes of the jungle, the prospect of disease and death was not only probable, but highly likely. Leave that for the poor unfortunate souls seeking a better life who didn't know what they were getting into. Wait, isn't that what happened to the indentured Indians who came to Jamaica? The Indians left their poor economy in hopes of a better life in Jamaica, even while Jamaicans were leaving a poor economy in hopes of a better life elsewhere. And so the cycle goes, even today.

Walter Boothe worked as a stoker at the railway. This was considered one of the skilled jobs, for which the salary was decent and free roundtrip passage had been offered. As it turned out, life was more difficult than many hopeful migrants had imagined not only because of the physical working conditions, but also the financial. Fraud, bribery and politics rendered the entire scheme unprofitable and unable to compete with the banana industry, which was just beginning to boom in Costa Rica.

I don't know the exact year that our young

couple went abroad, nor do I know exactly when they returned, but I do know that their daughter Daisy had been born in Jamaica in July 1904, and two babies were born in Costa Rica almost a year to the day later. Before they went to Costa Rica, the family had lived in Bluefields, Westmoreland, close to both sets of grandparents. By the time they returned, baby Daniel was with them (his twin sister had died shortly after birth), and the family was able to own land in Retirement, St. Elizabeth.

Their sixth child, Franklin, was born in Jamaica in 1908, so we know they spent less than four years abroad. My mother's first cousin, "Uncle" Earl, said that Walter had a horse-and-buggy vehicle and was well-respected. Upon his return from Costa Rica, he had become a "jailhouse lawyer", meaning that, although he did not have any formal law training, Walter fancied himself as being educated enough to understand and explain the law to his friends and neighbours who may have needed legal assistance or advice.

Walter "Old Boothe" Boothe - my most enduring family member thus far!

I did find evidence of that in the newspapers of the day. Old Boothe made various appearances in court, on behalf of himself as well as others, for petty charges like opening his shop on Good Friday, breaching the main roads law, and a property dispute. He ran for office in 1926 as Sanitary Inspector for the St. Thomas division of Westmoreland. The St. Thomas division related to the Bluefields area. He lost his bid for the position when the votes were counted, but it gave me some idea of the kind of social status that he had acquired, or at least imagined he had acquired. At any rate, Walter managed to establish himself as the family patriarch, and is credited with paving the way for many of my family members to be able to own property or to receive an education.

This seems to be what most Jamaicans intended when they left for greener pastures. They wanted to go away, earn some money, and return soon enough to enjoy some of their hard work, and maybe even climb the social ladder. They sought ways to avoid having to struggle in Jamaica for the rest of their lives. Some got other ideas after they left, or their circumstances may have changed, but overall, that seems to have been the aim of most, from what I've learnt.

In that sense, it seems to me that they were not that different from Jamaicans today. My daughter shared with me recently that from her observation, immigrants often don't reap the benefits or success they dream of, but their children do, and she may be right. I have heard of 'the American Dream' – an idea that anyone, regardless of where they were born or what class they were born into, can attain their own version of success in a society where upward mobility is possible for everyone. This proverbial American Dream is achieved through sacrifice, risk-taking and hard work, and not by chance. Well, my question is, how is this different from the Jamaican Dream, or in fact, the dream or ideal of any people?

Meet Clarinda, the Babymaker

As mentioned before, my maternal ancestors seem to have had rather large families. Walter's wife Agnes herself was one of 10 children, but it was her grandfather, Archibald Anglin, who piqued my interest.

The main reason was that Archibald was born on the Orange Grove plantation in Westmoreland, and was, for a considerable part of my research, the only specific link I had to a family member who had lived during the era of slavery.

Before 1834, there were no birth marriage or death records of individuals not considered free in Jamaica. This was because they were considered the property of whoever purchased them, or their parents (in the same way you might think of your pet, or an item of furniture). True, the African slave trade was abolished by British Parliament, effective January 1, 1808. But this only meant that slave trading between Africa and the British West Indies colonies was no longer allowed. It was still permissible to transport enslaved people from one colony to the other.

In order to enforce this rule, an act of Parliament was passed in 1816 requiring plantation owners to keep a register (detailed list) on the names and numbers of people working on their property. This would prevent further trading from Africa, as there had to be a record of the arrival and departure of each person by name. Therefore, effective June 1817 and until 1834, Jamaican landowners maintained "Slave Registers" every three years which documented the birth, death and sale of each worker, the names of infants' mothers, and the person they had been purchased from or sold to, if applicable. All this was duly witnessed by an attorney, in the same way a businessowner today might record the acquisition or disposal of an asset.

When I found Agnes Boothe's grandfather Archie on the 1817 register, he was only 12 years old and had already been given a Christian first and last name. He was named Archibald Anglin. His mother, Clarinda, was 35 years old, and being listed as "Creole" meant that she was born in the West Indies. Archie had three younger brothers named Quashie, Nimrod and Cuffee. In 1817 they were nine, six and two years old respectively. Their sister Becky was apparently born some time after June 1817 as indicated by subsequent registers. The Akan names of Quashie and Cuffee may suggest Ghanaian origin, but I learned not to assume that, since plantation owners were known to name workers whatever they chose, without regard for African naming conventions or customs.

I followed Clarinda's story for several years and realized that she had at least nine children in total, roughly two and a half years apart. None of her children were listed as mulatto, nor any variation of such. Were all Clarinda's children fathered by the same person? It was impossible for me to know, as children were recorded with the names of their mother, not their father, on the register. Possibly the feeling was that in the event of a trade it was necessary to keep a child with its mother for the immediate physical and emotional well-being of both, but it was less important to do so for the father, and therefore not important to even know who he was. Many people today feel that the normalizing of this arrangement accounts for the chronic absenteeism found among Jamaican fathers today. I found myself hoping that in spite of the unfair situation in which they found themselves, Clarinda's children had the presence of both their parents. In practice, mothers of six or more children were exempt from field labour on plantations, and Clarinda may have benefitted from this.

A significant event which many Jamaicans have heard of was the Christmas Day Rebellion of 1831. On that occasion, an estimated 60,000 of Jamaica's 300,000 enslaved population mobilized themselves against the establishment of the day. Archibald would have been 26 years old at the time of that uprising. The revolt started in St. James and quickly spread to Trelawny, Hanover, Westmoreland and even as far as St. Elizabeth.

Fields and buildings were set ablaze and 14 landowners or their representatives were killed. Troops retaliated by killing some 200 in the 11 days that followed. By May 1832, an additional 300 enslaved people had been executed for participation in the uprising, or for minor offenses. Samuel Sharpe was publicly hanged for his role in instigating this affair in what is now called "Sam Sharpe Square", the centre of the city of Montego Bay. In truth Sharpe had actually organized a peaceful sit out – workers would not go back to work until landowners agreed to granting better working conditions – but a strong message had to be sent to any future rebels, and someone had to be held responsible for those 14 deaths.

I would imagine that the age of 26 would have been prime fighting age. So how had Archibald managed to escape this tumultuous event with his life intact? Obviously, I cannot be sure, but I located documents wherein estate owners made claims relating to buildings which had been destroyed by fire during the revolt. I noticed with interest – and mild surprise – that Orange Grove was not among them. Does this mean that the workers there saw no need to participate, or does it mean that that they hadn't gotten organized enough to get involved? Were they so afraid of the consequences that they chose to quietly celebrate the goings-on while pretending to defend their enslavers, or had the revolt been effectively stamped out by the time the news got to them in the hills of Westmoreland?

William Anglin was listed as owner of Orange Grove plantation at the time of the uprising, and he was a captain of the Westmoreland militia, so maybe he had the army at his disposal. It may have been that his workers knew that they wouldn't stand a chance.

The biggest clue, though, was from the memoir of Grace Elizabeth Pinnock, who was nine years old at the time of that event. Her father Phillip Pinnock, owner of neighbouring Shafston Estate, had suddenly died just a few months before the uprising in question. Shortly before her death in 1897, Grace recounted and documented the events that led up to her family's departure from Jamaica, where she had been born, to England, the birthplace of her mother. She remembered idyllic days spent dancing Jonkunnu with 'the Negroes', as she called them, while her mother would join in by making music for the dancing. Grace wrote about the movement and rhythm of the dancers as "a natural grace and refinement of manner that is rarely attained even by the highest culture".

She also recalled the anxiety and fear when the news of the revolt reached her now-widowed mother, who wasn't quite sure if she could trust the assurances of her own enslaved people that they would physically defend the Pinnock family against any aggressors, and their proposal that the family should remain upstairs throughout the night, while they would stand guard on the lower floors to protect the home and its inhabitants. The children were put to bed fully dressed to enable a swift departure the next morning. There was no attack, and as soon as practical the following day, Mrs. Pinnock and her two sons and two daughters set off to the town of Savanna-la-Mar to seek refuge. The plan was that in the event of matters getting much worse, they could quickly make an escape by sea using one of the nearby ships.

For several days they watched and waited for news regarding the property they had left behind, fearing the worst. At last, with martial law enacted and guns overpowering machetes, the plantocracy regained their dominance and the damage was assessed. The Africans had promised Mrs. Pinnock that they would bury her valuables in order to protect them. Grace, her mother and eldest brother George noted with total awe and disbelief upon their return that nothing at the Shafston estate was missing, "nothing was even scratched." Grace had earlier in her memoir declared that on their own and adjoining plantations, the estate owner was considered a friend and counsellor. This challenged my own view that there was a natural antagonism between the two groups. At the very least, what I was learning from Grace was that the relationships were complicated.

Whether or not the Pinnocks' workers viewed them as friends, it does put some context to the atmosphere at Shafston and the neighbouring properties, which included Bluefields, Content,

Culloden, and the one with which I was primarily concerned, Orange Grove. In the months that followed, the extent of the damages was officially estimated. I found it noteworthy that none of the above-mentioned plantations claimed any damage to their properties and that may be a somewhat roundabout explanation for why Archibald was still alive, if not well, in 1838 at the end of apprenticeship. There appears to have been no attempt at rebellion on the Orange Grove plantation.

The events of 1831-1832 led the British government to re-examine the viability of using forced labour as a basis for their economy. In England, they were finding it more and more difficult to justify tens of thousands of men, women and children working in chains, especially at the risk of British lives. A decision was made to gradually "phase out" the practice of slavery. On August 28, 1833 the Emancipation Act was passed. It declared that on August 1, 1834, slaves in British colonies under the age of six years old were freed but older ones would continue to work for 40 hours per week in exchange for accommodation, food, clothing and medical attendance. They would also be given a portion of land to grow their own provisions. They were allowed to work for pay if they so chose, for any time in excess of their mandatory 40 hours. With these funds, it was suggested, they could purchase their full freedom. This system of "apprenticeship" was to last for the next seven years, and was scheduled to come to an end in 1841.

The whole idea was a failure. Plantation owners resented having to negotiate hours of work with people they basically considered to be beneath them, and they saw no reason to feed, house and clothe anyone who was not contributing to production. Consequently, in some places, nursing women, as well as the aged and infirm who were previously exempt from field labour, were sent to work in the field. Furthermore, though estate owners were not legally allowed to mistreat their workers, in practice, it was generally viewed as a period during which they should attempt to squeeze out every last bit of compulsory labour before freedom set in. So for some, things actually got worse.

I do not know how Clarinda fared. She may have changed her name as many did when full emancipation came earlier than expected in 1838, which would explain why I was unable to track her down after that date. She may have even gone to one of the free villages established by emancipated workers where they tried to be self-sufficient rather than depend on the wider economy.

The records show that Archibald was still living in Orange Grove in 1838. By then he was 33 years old and had started a family there. Trees created by other family members suggest that he may have fathered a total of six children, beginning in 1835. The records which I have found and confirmed include four children and their mother Sarah. There were Archibald Junior, Thomas Roland, Albert and Elizabeth. By 1840, Archibald was working as a carpenter in the district of Porters in Westmoreland.

It was Archibald's son, Thomas Roland Anglin, who became Agnes' father. Agnes grew up and married Walter Boothe ("Old Boothe") in 1895. She was eight years old when her grandfather Archibald died. Did he tell her what he had lived through? Maybe she would have been too young. But certainly, her father Thomas would have known. He died at the age of 85 years in 1923.

I imagine that Thomas' children and grandchildren learned a great deal about what life was really like for Clarinda, Archie and the rest of the family. I reflected on the fact that Grace and her brother George Pinnock had been careful to preserve their memories and their perspectives by writing them down for their children and for us, which forms the basis for what many of us believe about their time. It can be argued that it was true for them, and in that sense, it was history, at least from their perspective. Clarinda and millions of others had little opportunity to do the same. They shared as many facts as they could through oral history, but emotions and opinions are not so easily transmitted, and after the first generation or two, are usually distorted, watered down or entirely lost. My task of trying to piece their lives together through fragmented bits and pieces of their stories, is an attempt, however feeble, to give voice to millions who have been silenced for hundreds of years.

The Greenfields and Rileys

One thing I learned very early in this project is that it is impossible to separate family history from family drama. Working on uncovering the past will naturally re-open some wounds and maybe even a few secrets.

I think working on this project has made me something of a philosopher. As I went along on this journey, I decided that I would accept all my family drama without anger or resentment. The facts are what they are, and I couldn't change that. No amount of bitterness, judgment or tears could reverse time. Instead, I decided to use my family's stories as roadmaps to understanding why things are the way they are, not just for my family, but for the society in which I live. This goes for your family too. The patchwork of alliances and enmities which cause you stress, or which you can't understand, or which have "always been" that way, are really the result of coincidences, tragedies, mishaps, lies and deceits which shape your family relationships. My advice is to just deal with it and try not to make the same mistakes yourself.

So when I needed to talk about what made them so, I learned to talk about the "shameful" bits in a straightforward manner. Every family has them, and the actions you and I take today will be dissected and perhaps criticized by our grandchildren and beyond.

My father's aunt Inez lived about 20 minutes away from my home in Canada and though I had just moved to Canada a little over two years before, I never got around to visiting her until I started this project. My father had always insisted that I should "look her up", and when we were packing for the big move in 2014, he wrote her phone number down and I assured him I would call. I did call within a few months of my arrival and made the usual promises to visit, but the excuses were always the same – "the roads are too icy so we'll do it in the summer", "hectic work schedule", "I won't be able to find my way", etc., etc. Even my daughter kept insisting, "Mom, we really should talk to the oldest person in our family." Of course, her logic was sound; it just made sense to talk to the elders before memories faded or opportunities were missed. But it wasn't until the project started taking shape and I needed some real answers that we made a date of it and went to visit Aunt Inez and her daughter "Aunty Scottie" one Monday afternoon.

It was, appropriately, on Canada's Family Day, a holiday specifically celebrating families and encouraging them to spend time together, that we arranged to make the visit. Aunt Inez represented for me a crucial — and in some ways painful — link between my father and his now-deceased mother.

The thing is, my father hadn't been raised by his mother. He never knew her until he was a grown man. What I did know of my grandmother was that she was a very educated woman. My father had no stories to tell about his mother as a girl or a young woman. He told me of one single episode when he remembered meeting her for the first time as a boy of eight or nine years old. He remembers she said to him, "Hello, young man."

"Hello, ma'am."

She ran her hand through his hair. "What happened to your nice hair?"

"I don't know, ma'am."

That's the only time he remembers speaking with her until about 20 years later when, married to the most determined woman he had ever met — my mother — he started on a journey to find the mystery woman who had brought him into the world. By doing a bit of detective work, my parents found out her married name which was by no means uncommon. And what did they do? Using the telephone directory, they went about narrowing down the possibilities and calling each and every one of them. After several weeks of this process, she was found.

I'm told that once connected, their relationship was strained, at first. But things improved over time. They improved to the point where I remember that starting when I was about seven or eight years old, we would take yearly trips to Kingston, and we would stay there overnight. Her husband, whom my father called "Dad", was a kind and caring man. He never made us feel like outsiders and we looked forward to seeing him on each visit.

With my grandmother things were a bit different. Maybe it was more a result of her personality and less of the history of the relationship, but I remember tip-toeing around her and feeling like I had done something wrong by being there. I didn't know the back-story then, so I don't think that it was my own self-consciousness that caused this feeling. Now that I do know the back-story, I don't really like talking about it. It makes me sad. But more than that, it makes me a bit angry, I think. I believe it makes me angrier than it makes my father. Maybe he just doesn't show it, or maybe he has already worked his way through the grief, guilt and anger that comes with feelings of rejection and had accepted the lack of relationship with his mother long before. Getting to know her and being a part of her life would represent an improvement over what he had already dealt with for many years.

When I was a girl, I would get glimpses of what it must have been like for my father as a young boy growing up in rural St. James. He was raised by his father's mother, as also happened in my mother's case. He told me that there was a radio program called "Sunday Contact" (I later found out that it still airs on Jamaican radio) where old friends, missing family members, schoolmates who had lost contact could basically reach out by giving details of who they were, who they were looking for and how you could get in touch with them. Factors such as migration and lack of modern communication technology such as internet and telephones made this the most efficient search method for people looking to locate their long-lost friends and relatives. Think of it as Ancestry.com or Facebook for the 1960s.

My dad admitted to me once that sometimes late on Sunday nights he would go under his covers and turn the radio really low, hoping to hear that his mother was searching for him. He never did. His grandmother, obviously concerned about him getting his hopes up, would chide him and tell him to turn the radio off and go to bed, hoping no doubt to spare him from more disappointment, Sunday after Sunday.

I am a very understanding and forgiving person. I have even been accused of being overly forgiving. I understand to a limited extent the social climate of the 1950s in Jamaica. I accept that the rules were different for a young black girl from the country. Having a child out of wedlock was shameful and was a sentence to a life of peasantry and childbearing. The child's father would have no such shackle imposed upon him unless that was his choice. If she wanted to make a change to her circumstances, she had to make a hard decision at the expense of someone's happiness – her child's or her own. So I get that, and I don't judge her for leaving my father in the care of his grandparents. But I would be lying if I said I wasn't angry that she didn't give him the privilege of knowing her. Granted, I don't have all the facts, but was there no middle ground?

I got another glimpse into my grandmother Elgetha's life when I located two sets of newspaper articles:

At 14 years old, she was accepted as a member of the Children's Corner Club, a morning concert at the Carib Theatre in Kingston. My dad's sister confirms that Elgetha was much more well-read than others in her small Hanover district. She had aspirations of better and greater things than her little country life in Riverside. Those aspirations must have seemed to be slipping away when only two years later, she was in court as a witness in a murder case.

According to her testimony, Elgetha had gone to the movies in Lucea with her friend Petra on Monday, May 15, 1950. Petra had apparently been involved with a policeman who had only gotten married in August of the previous year. After the movies that night, Elgetha and Petra met up with the officer at Riley Bridge as was previously arranged. Elgetha testified that at that point she left them together under a tree. Somehow, the officer's wife had gotten wind of this rendezvous and confronted the pair. The short version of the story is that the confrontation led to a very nasty brawl in which the policeman's 19-year-old wife was struck with a stone, slapped in the face and chest, dragged across the street and had her head bashed against the bridge. She was rescued by another policeman who drove up on the scene. He put her in his car and took her to her mother's home. She died in hospital the next day.

After a number of hearings held between October 24 and 31, both defendants were acquitted on the basis of the pathologist's report stating that it was "unlikely" and "far-fetched" that a slight girl of 17 years old could inflict a wound which would cause a skull fracture. He also concluded that the backhand stroke given by her husband would not have resulted in a fracture or a concussion, despite two eyewitness accounts claiming to have seen him bang her head against the bridge wall. The jury acquitted both accused.

I don't know how all of this impacted Elgetha. I imagine she was shaken up, but I have never heard anyone else from the family mention it. My aunt and uncle were shocked to learn of it, and I chose not to ask my grandaunt.

Elgetha wanted to leave Hanover behind. This may have been not only the country life, the lack of opportunities and lack of sophistication, but also the memories and the mistakes. The shiny, new, picket-fence life could not accommodate both realities. I suppose she wrestled with her decision some nights, but I reason this way: if you're already lying to yourself and the world by denying the existence of your child, how difficult would it be to invent some other excuse to be a benevolent friend or relative who occasionally takes a trip to the "country" to see to your distant relative's well-being? At least this would establish some kind of relationship. Wouldn't pretending to be a cousin be a much more forgiving lie than the one where you told yourself that the child you bore never existed? Some questions will never be answered; my grandmother died in 2007. My best bet in 2017, was talking to her big sister, Inez. Maybe she could shed some light. Maybe she could help me justify some of the things that just didn't seem to make sense.

I started my interview by telling my grandaunt that I was doing this project for my daughter. This family tree is her family tree, but it had morphed into so much more. Her response was the same as all my other interviewees – excited about the family tree but sure that she wouldn't be able to contribute much because she really didn't know that much. That's okay, I assured her, the same way I always assured the others. "You know far more than you think you do." In Aunt Inez' case this was truer than any of the other branches of the tree, since my initial draft only had one maternal limb from my father, and that was his mother's name. We did not know the names of her parents nor have any little anecdotes that naturally occur in family histories. So I convinced Aunt Inez that anything she could remember would be greatly appreciated.

She spoke fondly and at length about their

mother, my great-grandmother, Mrs. Eva Greenfield (née Riley). Up until that time, I wasn't aware of any Rileys in my family. As I mentioned, my father grew up not knowing much about his mother's family. I found out from document research that Eva's parents were Daniel Riley and Isabella Stewart-Riley, and that Daniel's father was Richard Riley. Daniel was born in 1861 and while I didn't find Richard's date of birth, my general estimate would be around 1830. If so, it would explain why I couldn't find an official birth document for him, as full freedom was not granted until 1838 and enslaved people did not have official records until then. It also explains why he may have taken the name Riley. There was a large sugar plantation which went by the name of Riley's Estate in Hanover. The "Riley" area still exists today, and has landmarks such as the Riley Bridge, which runs over Riley River (better known as Lucea West River). Riley's estate was about two miles southeast of Lucea, and Eaton was a further mile or so south of Riley. Daniel got married and raised his family in Eaton.

Miss Eva had two children before marrying my great-grandfather Derrious or Richard Greenfield. Aunt Inez said, "His name was Derrious Greenfield, or Perry. When you are doing your research, look for Perry."

I was confused about that. What did the name Perry have to do with Greenfield? I didn't press for more information because I wasn't sure it was relevant. I scribbled it in my notebook and I'm glad I did.

Sure enough, when I did my online records search, I found a marriage record for Richard Alexander Pirie, married to Eva Riley in Hanover on May 21, 1932. That seemed straightforward enough; my great-grandfather's name was Richard Pirie. Not so fast. The name of Richard's father was shown on the marriage certificate as William Greenfield. I wrinkled my eyebrows at that. Why would he have a different surname from that of his father? But it was his death certificate, signed by none other than his daughter Elgetha Greenfield (my grandmother) that really sent me into a tailspin. By then, his name was Derrious Perry Greenfield. So when he got married, his name was Richard Pirie, and by the time he died he became Derrious Greenfield? I didn't understand it and my best link, his daughter — my grand-aunt Inez — didn't know enough to clarify matters. I moved on – not happy, not satisfied, but no one else seemed to know or care, so what choice did I have?

Together, Eva and Richard/Derrious had four children: Newton, Inez, Eugene, and my grandmother Elgetha (the youngest). Derrious died in 1949 when he was only 47 years old and this may explain why Aunt Inez was not able to give me a great deal of family background about her father and his family. I remember going to Chambers Pen with my parents when I was about 11 or 12 years old to visit Uncle Eugene. It was the only time I remember meeting him.

Of course, I had only a vague idea of who he was. I knew he was a relative of my father's, and since we called him "Uncle Genie" I could hazard a guess as to the nature of the relationship, but for some reason at the time I imagined that he was related to my father's paternal family. I think this might have been because some of the old-timers in the small community who had caught sight of my younger brother who was about four or five years old, remarked at how much he was "Tailor's own self!" "Tailor Clarke" was my dad's paternal grandfather, so I naturally assumed all these years that Uncle Eugene was a member of my father's paternal family, the Clarke side. It never occurred to me that both of my grandparents had ties in the same tiny community.

In retrospect I should have known that Uncle Genie was not a Clarke relative, because my Aunt Cathy and her family had also come to visit him, and she was my dad's maternal half-sister. But when you are a kid you don't really think about these things with anything more than surface curiosity. At least, I didn't. I now realize that the reason those old-timers knew both sides of my father's family was that they were both originally from that area. You will learn more about my grandparents Elgetha and Lynden later.

Uncle Genie had all but lost his eyesight when I visited as a child. I remember that the soil on that little hill where the old house was, was quite different from anything I had ever seen before. It was like burgundy sheets, or layers of dirt, rather than being crumb-like. There was a small secondary structure next to the house which seemed to be a storage area or shed, but may easily have been an outhouse or something of that nature. I remember overhearing with interest that despite his blindness, Uncle Genie was practically self-sufficient, able to cook and do a little farming on his own. He died in 2007 at the age of 83.

My own research uncovered two additional generations of Greenfields, those of Derrious' father and grandfather, William and George Greenfield respectively.

Almost a whole year later, I was relating my confusion about Derrious' name change to my dad's maternal half-brother and he offhandedly said, "Oh, yes; a lady took him in and she kind of adopted him. You know nothing was official those days so he kind of got their name."

What?!

So we are NOT related to the Greenfields by blood? Sigh. And the name Pirie seems to have died out; I cannot seem to locate anyone with that name, except one – John Pirie. Buried in 1796 in Hanover. No further information available. It is entirely possible that this name may have turned into "Perry" over time, as there are no shortages of that name in Jamaica, even in Hanover.

I learned from my grandaunt that Miss Eva raised her children in rural Hanover around the

Chambers Pen/Askenish/Harvey River districts and we made small talk about sibling birth order, dates of birth and the like. Aunt Inez gave me copies of several carefully preserved photos of the great-grandmother I had never known nor heard about.

During our conversation, there was a long pause which signaled the presence of an elephant in the room. The time had come to talk about my own grandmother. I stated frankly that families get uncomfortable when speaking about such topics, but that I had basically already put two and two together. Furthermore, at almost 40 years of age in the year 2017, there was little to be kept secret from me right now. I asked my grandaunt, "Did you know when my father was born?"

She raised her head toward me, but it isn't quite accurate to say she looked at me. Rather, it seemed as though she were looking past me, through me, even. That was probably the look of memories coming back, or of Aunt Inez trying to think of some way to tell me what she had to say without hurting my feelings. It seemed like a very long pause, but it was really only about 10 seconds. Then she said quietly, "Yes."

She told the story of my grandmother, Elgetha, or "G" as they called her, living in Kingston. She said, "G used to tell everyone that her name was 'Elgetha' [hard "g" sound], but it was El-jee-tha!" She rolled her eyes. I chuckled inwardly at that. There was that sibling rivalry – as old as Cain and Abel! I pictured the young golden child, who got the opportunity to improve herself by getting an education in the big city, suddenly getting airs by changing the pronunciation of her name so that she didn't sound so "country" to her new friends. In fact, when she died a few years ago, my uncle posted a notice in the newspaper acknowledging several variations of her name, including "Elgitha, Elgeta," and the way she signed her name officially, "Elgetha".

I didn't communicate my amusement to my grandaunt, of course, since I didn't want that to become the focus of the story. So, as the narrative continued, Aunt Inez explained that "G" had gone to Kingston to further her education but as these stories seem to go, she ended up pregnant. Ironically, my grandfather was from a neighbouring district in Hanover, not too far from where my grandmother and her siblings grew up.

Aunt Inez said that she had come to know of the pregnancy (she didn't say how) and got to find out when the baby was born. A young man from their area who was a truck driver would often make trips to Kingston. He knew where G lived and offered to take Inez for a visit. Her face broke out into the broadest smile ever. "He was so pink. And his fingers were so long!" she exclaimed as she relived the moment. Then, in a few seconds, it was over. Her smile faded and she was back with me. Propriety, it seems, didn't allow her to say more. We chatted about other family members and she brought out an album and shared pictures of her mom (Eva), my grandmother (Elgetha) and my uncle, who is my dad's half-brother. He was born after Elgetha finished up school, got her degree, got married and lived in the proverbial house with the white picket fence in a decent Kingston/St. Andrew neighbourhood. So I guess you could say she made good for herself after all.

I am grateful for qualities like forgiveness and acceptance. My father is pretty close to his half-siblings. I am happy that despite the shaky past, Elgetha's siblings, children and even her husband happily welcomed us when they learned of the existence of my dad, and by extension, his children. I'm happy not because either party gained some material advantage by knowing the other, but emotionally, people crave answers to questions about origins and belonging. We all seem to be created with a desire to know where we are 'from', evidenced by a large money-making genealogy and ancestry industry. Taking away or withholding this knowledge leads to the frustrations we see depicted in the lives of adopted children, even if their adopted parents are warm, caring and affectionate.

My grandmother, Elgetha Greenfield - quite beautiful, if I say so myself!

We, the kids of the next generation, are also quite ready to move on and live normally with each other. My younger brothers are social media friends with all the cousins, and I have followed suit. It just feels right. As cousins, we do not speak about the past of three generations ago, even though most of us know that there were some unpleasant secrets. Should we? I'm not sure. What would it accomplish? Lots of uncomfortable conversations, for sure. Maybe even some defensiveness. Would it make us any closer? Probably not. In conversations with others outside of my family, I've concluded that this type of history is not that unusual at all.

Years ago, I didn't understand how my father could have had such a "good" surface relationship with his mother after everything that had happened. How could he not have been offended after being shut out of her life? Why had he sought her out? How could he have embraced her with open arms? Was he just naive? I recently heard someone express forgiveness this way: Forgiveness is not an emotion; it's a decision. You don't do it for the other person; you do it for yourself. Forgiveness allows you to let go of anger and bitterness, which make you sick and frankly, make you ugly. My father understood this even if he didn't express it this way. What a great lesson to teach a child! Thanks, Dad.

Clarke, and Other Too-Common Surnames

I was born with the last name Clarke. Nothing too significant there. According to the genealogy website forebears.io, that is the seventh most common Jamaican last name. For every 97 people, there's a Clarke in there. With a reported 29,000 people in a population of 3,000,000 sharing the name, it wasn't going to be easy to find any long-lost anyone.

My father was raised by his grandmother Estrianna Clarke. She died when I was five years old, but I do remember going to visit her a few times with my parents in the rural St. James district where my dad was raised.

We called her "Mother" and my parents told me that she gave me a goat. I don't remember much about the goat, but I do remember Mother. I remember that she always seemed very pleased to see me. She would have some little treat for me when I came to visit. I vaguely remember my very first bank account at Jamaica National Building Society being opened with some funds she gave to my dad for me. It was 75 Jamaican dollars. Suffice it to say, I liked "Mother".

But "Mother" had been born as Estrianna Campbell, not Clarke. She married Harold Clarke some time between 1920 and 1923. And where does the name "Campbell" rank on the list of common Jamaican surnames? Number four. That statistic means that roughly, for every 69 people in Jamaica, there's a Campbell in there. So, without any specific references, I wasn't likely to get any new information. That was okay; I mainly wanted to confirm whatever stories I had heard growing up.

My great-grandfather Harold was a tailor by trade, and that was what he was called by everyone in the area. My dad told us that Tailor was among the thousands of Jamaican workers who emigrated to post-independence Cuba to improve their economic lot in life. Advertisements were run in Jamaica's Daily Gleaner for cane cutters, shoemakers, domestic workers, tailors and the like.

My dad says that Harold was making uniforms for "the war", but he wasn't able to tell me which war. I don't have an accurate date of birth for Harold. He may have been somewhere between 19 and 23 years old at the time of World War I, so I am not sure whether I can say with any certainty what uniforms he was making. I do know that my grandaunt Delta (Tailor's daughter) was born in July 1923 and her birth certificate shows the name and dwelling place of her father as, "Harold Clarke, Cuba," and his profession as "Tailor." The birth certificate shows that during this time, his wife Estrianna stayed with her parents Edward and Jane Campbell in Riverside.

It seems that Harold got more than one stint in Cuba, because my granduncle Leon was born in 1925 in Jamaica, but Estrianna went through at least three pregnancies in Cuba, all after 1925. My dad told me that when he felt the time was right (or when he was able), Harold brought Estrianna over to Cuba, while Delta and Leon stayed in Catadupa, St. James with Harold's parents.

Estrianna gave birth to my grandaunt Gloria while she was living in Cuba, but when she became pregnant again (with my grandfather, as it turned out), she decided to return home, since living conditions in Cuba were difficult. She had, in fact, lost at least one baby there and the way my father tells it, Estrianna was adamant that she would not give birth to another child in that unpleasant environment.

My Cuban-born grandaunt Gloria is the only one of those siblings who is still alive at the time I am writing this. She recalls that she was about six years old when they left Cuba. That sounds about right. This means that the family left for Cuba sometime between 1925 and 1927, and returned to Jamaica around 1933.

My dad recently shared with me a Spanish phrase Estrianna had picked up while she was in Cuba – "Pobrecito! No tiene dinero, pero sí yo tengo." He had a vague idea of what it meant and asked me to confirm. I told him that it basically translated to, "Poor thing! He/she has no money, but I do." I don't know in what context his grandmother had heard this phrase, but obviously she heard it often enough to know it well. It is said that you can learn a lot about a society or culture by its words. These are the words that "Mother" took back from Cuba almost 90 years ago, and my father remembers them today. I had never thought that my dad was making up this chapter of his grandparents' lives, but it felt good to have that interesting bit of history confirmed by documents.

Leaving Cuba at that time was a good call by Estrianna. Between August 1933 and 1937, Cuba experienced a violent political upheaval led by Fulgencio Batista. This had been preceded by a collapse in the price of sugar, the industry around which Cuba had built almost its entire economy. The collapse of the sugar industry itself had come about as a result of the Wall Street crash of 1929.

A letter to the editor in the Jamaica Gleaner newspaper in 1921 complained of the racism and high rate of unemployment faced by Jamaicans who had gone to Cuba to earn a living. What was worse, though, was that even though many of them wanted to return home, they were stuck there as they didn't have enough money to pay for their return passage. The writers were appealing to the government to look into the matter and come to the assistance of its citizens.

Estrianna returned to Jamaica ahead of Harold. With two children already being taken care of by her in-laws, she didn't want to add to the awkwardness by adding herself, a new baby in tow and another baby on the way to the equation. If Estrianna hadn't left when she did, quite possibly my father wouldn't have been born. Many Jamaicans ended up being stuck in Cuba due to the many years of unrest which began in August 1933. My grandfather Lynden, the baby she was pregnant with at the time, was born in Jamaica on September 7, 1933.

She told Harold that she intended to buy a piece of land with the money they had saved up. She came to learn of seven acres of land available in John's Hall, St. James. She told Harold about it, but he was not thrilled about the idea. He wanted to return and set up a shop as a tailor. John's Hall was still underdeveloped at the time and wouldn't provide enough opportunities to sell suits. According to family legend, Estrianna told him, "Alright then, if you hear of anything before the closing date, you let me know. Otherwise I am buying that land."

Harold didn't hear of any other land for sale, so that is how she came to purchase that farming property for £300 in rural St. James. At any rate, John's Hall was much closer to Montego Bay than

Catadupa, which no doubt made it easier for my father to move to the city years later and raise his family there.

That is how my grandfather Lynden came to be raised in John's Hall, St. James. But since his parents Harold and Estrianna still had family ties in Riverside, Hanover, they would regularly take Leon, Delta, Gloria and Lynden there. As a result of this, the kids knew the area and the families there well, and they formed friendships. Now, I don't know much about my grandfather's childhood, but based on what my father and his aunt say, interesting things started happening between Lynden and a young lady by the name of Elgetha, or "G".

Elgetha had already had one baby when she was 20 years old. Needless to say, G's mother was not pleased to learn of this new relationship. She took steps to put a stop to it. Since G was academically inclined, she arranged to send her off to college in the big city, Kingston, over 100 miles away. So G goes off to get an education and, crisis averted, right? Wrong. Evidently, the relationship continued and two years to the date of her first child's birth, G gave birth to a baby boy. She kept the entire matter from everyone back home. She was living at her older brother Newton's home in Kingston, but she swore him to secrecy and, I suppose, he took the position that it was none of his business so he didn't let on to anyone.

G's older sister had always been in the habit of

making trips to visit her whenever she got a chance. On one occasion in the spring of 1955 she made her usual arrangements to go into Kingston and when she got to her brother Newton's home, she called at Elgetha's door. Elgetha responded but didn't let her in right away. Instead, she told her to wait a while. This was curious; was there a young man in there with her? When the door finally opened, lo and behold! Not a young man, but a baby! A baby?! What was the meaning of this? Elgetha told her older sister that if she breathed a word to anyone, she could stop coming to visit and never expect to hear from her again. That threat aside, Inez asked her younger sister what the plan was. Both parents were only 22 years old and in no position, financial or otherwise, to raise a child.

Elgetha did have a plan, and it was this: she would tell Lynden's older sister, Delta, to let the Clarkes in John's Hall know what had happened. Ask Lynden's mom to take the child and raise him there. My dad recounts the story he was told: upon hearing the news, his grandmother Estrianna, or "Mother" as he came to know her, walked three miles to catch the bus into Kingston. Many hours later, she arrived in the city and made her way to Jonestown where she met the new arrival. She got back to Catadupa in the late hours of the night, with her little pink grandson in tow.

My dad doesn't know who was aware of his mother's secret before he was taken to live with his grandparents. Did his father's family know about him all along? We don't know.

Thus it happened that my father was raised by his paternal grandparents. But mostly his grandmother. His grandfather Harold died in 1966 when my father was 11 years old. His father Lynden became an educated man and worked in the Jamaica Forestry Department as a bookkeeper. It was considered a decent job with good benefits. It involved extensive traveling to different parts of the island, and he was provided with a house, a horse and an office. Lynden soon took a wife, and my father lived with them briefly before moving back to live with his grandmother. He didn't give me many details of the time when he lived with his father, nor why he moved back to St. James, but he did miss living with him. My dad has inherited his love of gardening from my grandfather, and speaks fondly of what he learned during the short time he lived with him. He takes pride in his flower and vegetable gardens and proudly shows off the various varieties of specially-grafted mangoes growing from a single tree.

Lynden and his wife soon started their own family and, as was the common dream at the time, started making plans to emigrate to England. Eventually, my dad's father, stepmother and paternal half-siblings left for the United Kingdom and began their new lives there around 1966. My father remembers the year because there was a cut-off age to apply for children to join their parents, and that was the year he would have no longer qualified, being the eldest child. I get a bit emotional every time he relates this story to me. I think about the sadness and loneliness of a 14-year-old whose closest family members were now all gone, and who was left to ponder some very deep questions at such a young age. And yet, if he had gone, he would not have had the chance to meet my mother. And you would not be reading this narrative.

My grandfather Lynden's wife, who is still alive, recently shared with my brother, who incidentally now lives in the UK, that life was quite difficult in 1960s England for a West Indian migrant family. What is more, they lived in Yorkshire, an area which had little to no cultural or ethnic diversity compared with London or Birmingham. They experienced blatant racial discrimination, and my grandfather, who had hoped to continue his profession by working as a tree surgeon (arboriculturist), was sorely disappointed as he was not even considered for this job for which he was more than qualified. With a family to feed and bills to pay, he accepted what work was available and eventually became a bus conductor.

More and more, I ponder the true accident of my existence, and I am humbled by my, or anyone's, lack of "right" to be here. There is a poem "Desiderata," by Max Ehrmann which proclaims everyone's right to be here, but I believe that the privilege I have of contemplating, objecting, debating and demanding anything is only due to some random incident or long-ago decision made by someone who really didn't do it with me specifically in mind at all. And yet, there are others who might have made a greater contribution than I have, who died as infants, who were stillborn or were simply never conceived because their would-be parents never met, or some other seemingly innocuous act. Makes you think, doesn't it?

Soldiers, Saddlers and Scotsmen

The Buckleys of St. Catherine

My husband has convinced himself over the years that he has "undiluted" African blood (whatever that means), with no evidence of this so-called fact other than the dark shade of his skin. He has conveniently ignored the fact that the tell-tale waves in his hair (as opposed to my coily hair) suggest otherwise, and like many Jamaicans he concludes that shades of skin colour are a direct indication of one's African-ness or lack thereof. I admit that to a lesser degree, I did believe that this ancestral project would lead me to some conclusive evidence of which ancestor(s) of mine "caused" my decidedly yellow skin-tone. It really wasn't that clear-cut at all. I did uncover little clues, but eventually it became such a low priority once I got to learn the really important stuff that in the end, it really didn't matter.

I started my interviews of my daughter's paternal relatives at the easiest starting point – her father. The name Buckley is not a very common one in Jamaica. It isn't rare, but I'm usually asked to repeat or spell it when I introduce myself. Many people assume I said the more commonly-known Buchanan, Bucknor or Buckingham. One thing that became apparent very quickly was that the Buckleys were predominantly, if not exclusively, based in the east of the island. That supported the conclusion I had drawn ever since I took on the name almost 20 years ago. However, I met my husband in the most westerly parish (Westmoreland), and he was the first Buckley I ever met.

I learned that my now-deceased father-in-law Aston Buckley was originally from St. Catherine, but my husband didn't know any of his extended family members on his father's side. When I first learned of this, I thought it strange, but now I think it is absolutely bizarre. My husband grew up with both his parents, and to some extent it makes sense that a small child might not be that curious about his extended family members, but I think I would have been quite curious as I got older. By the time he turned 15 years old, his father developed a terminal illness and that gave everyone other things to worry about, I suppose. I'm just sorry that my husband and his siblings didn't know enough about the Buckleys to have a relationship with their cousins, aunts and uncles. It might have been rather interesting.

Unfortunately, I never met my father-in-law since he died the year before I met my husband. Interviewing my husband for this book was particularly difficult because, having lost his father in death at such a young age, and really, losing him even before that to a cruel and painful disease, left many questions unanswered – questions which no doubt would have been answered in the natural course of time if Mr. Aston Buckley had lived a few more years, at least. He died in 1995 and I met my husband about two years later.

A place in St. Catherine called Harewood seems to be Ground Zero for the Buckleys who are connected to this family, and Aston's grandfather William Duncan Buckley lived there in the mid-to-late 1800s. William and his wife Grace Ann raised their son Philemon and his siblings there.

As a young man, Philemon was among the volunteers from Jamaica, Barbados, Guyana and other Caribbean countries who chose to fight in World War I. He served with the 7th Battalion of the British West Indies Regiment in France. I managed to locate the war diary of that particular battalion by taking advantage of the free access to the online British National Archives offered due to the COVID-19 pandemic. The commanding officer wrote about the daily journey starting from June 1, 1917 when they set sail from Jamaica, and continued to chronicle the daily events of life on the battlefield until the battalion was moved to Italy in December 1917. I read with quiet heartbreak of the heavy shelling and frightening casualties which befell these youngsters from Jamaica, Guyana, Barbados and other Caribbean countries. Quite a number of them were barely 20 years old. Many died from pneumonia as the cold, wet European winter began. Thousands who survived the 1917 winter would not survive the spring which arrived a few months later, as the

Spanish influenza pandemic swept through the army and went on to claim over 50 million lives worldwide, more than those killed at war. Philemon returned home alive, but with permanent hearing loss and two British War and Victory medals to show for his service.

Back in Jamaica, Philemon started working as a carpenter and met Gladys Saddler. She was the daughter of well-known beekeeper Maximillan Saddler in Braeton, St. Catherine. Mr. Maxi, as he was known, had the biggest house in their small St. Catherine village. He also had a horse and buggy and a small Ford truck which he would use to transport barrels of honey to the parish capital, Spanish Town, about five miles away. Despite what seemed to be a somewhat privileged upbringing in this rural community, Gladys found herself unmarried and pregnant at the age of 18 years. The birth of her son was registered by her father, Maxi, but baby Hartland died seven months later. Though there was no last name listed on his birth certificate (suggesting that his parents were unmarried), his death certificate showed the last name "Braham". By the time of her baby's death, Gladys had moved from the family home in Braeton to King Street in Spanish Town.

Philemon and Gladys got married in Spanish Town, St. Catherine in 1926. Their first two children, Harold and Vendeletia, died as infants, but they went on to have eight more children, including Aston. Aston was the second surviving child and was born in 1932. He was raised along with his siblings at 14 Railway Lane in St. Catherine. He became a carpenter like his father and at some point in the 1970s, he moved to Westmoreland where the tourism industry in Negril was developing quickly and with it, the construction of hotels. Being a carpenter by trade, he made a good living making furniture for hotels.

That part was easy enough to understand. Since the beginning of history, populations have migrated for better work, food and living conditions. The mystery here is this: Aston Buckley, who was by all accounts one of the most generous, benevolent and principled men around, had older children in Kingston, but my husband never knew of them.

Of course, I have questioned my husband's own lack of curiosity as a child, especially as a teenager, but I suppose those were different times. Children didn't really question their parents; if any information wasn't volunteered to you, well, that meant it was none of your business.

I made contact with a potential Buckley family member on social media as we seemed to share some family member names and places of residence. While not able to confirm anything, he mentioned that his father once told him about a cousin who had a dispute with his brothers about some land. After the falling-out, he moved to Westmoreland (the opposite end of the country), and they didn't hear from him again. Could that be our Aston? We don't know, but my husband and his siblings say their father would never haggle with anyone about land, so it may very well be that he would have left rather than take part in a prolonged land quarrel.

I was quite surprised to discover from the public records that Aston's father Philemon had been alive the entire time! In fact, he died in December 1995 – just a month after Aston passed away. Both were living at the family home on Railway Lane in Spanish Town at the time of death. Philemon's wife Gladys had died many years before, in 1967.

In reaching out to family members and other researchers like myself, I've concluded that every family has a keeper of family history – someone who takes an interest in, and is a kind of repository for the stories we all want from time to time. Some families have more than one. We go to those family members when we want to remember how Cousin So-and-so is related to us, or when Auntie So-and-so died.

I found out that my husband's younger sister had taken an interest in her aunts and uncles (her father's siblings), as well as her own older half-siblings, had made contact with them and kept in touch with them over the years. She herself seemed not to have gone into too much detail with them about the past and so I too thought it best to let sleeping dogs lie. This is a bit sad, because I believe that the older Buckley siblings are the keys to long-lost relatives and will finally help us to answer some of the questions that have been bugging me for the better part of 20 years. The issue, of course, is that feelings are involved. The generation that is directly impacted by decisions will usually find it most difficult to talk about these decisions without a bit of anger. With each successive generation, the hurt may sting a bit less, but then a bit of the accuracy and details may be lost.

I only hope that one day we will be able to figure out what to me, is a near 50-year-old mystery.

Saddlers and Beekeepers

Aston's mother Gladys was the middle child of Maximillian Saddler's three daughters, the other two being older sister Violet and younger sister Mabel.

The written records I found seem to indicate a comfortable enough upbringing. Mr. Maxi's honey business did well enough to employ people in the district, and having a motorized pickup van was no small thing in those days. In May 1918, he even made a generous donation of an organ to the Spanish Town Wesleyan Church. This gift was accepted by the same pastor who had performed his marriage to Birdena Tomlin seven months earlier. This was a pretty big deal. There was a newspaper write-up and everything.

Unfortunately, all was not well. By July 1920, Mr. Maxi and his wife Birdena had separated. She was now living at Old Hope Road in Kingston, and he took out a notice in the papers to that effect. I wasn't sure if Birdena was the mother of Gladys and her sisters, but I doubt it. Maxi and Birdena had gotten married when Violet was 17 or 18 years old, Gladys was about 11, and Mabel was about 10. Had their mother died? Who was she, and what was her story? That is still unknown to me.

What I do know is that within three years, Birdena had moved out and Gladys was pregnant with her first child by the time she was 18. Though Maxi and his wife were no longer living together, they did not get divorced. Birdena eventually died in 1931 and Maxi remarried in 1934. Was there animosity between the girls and their new stepmother? I don't know. She was the same age as Maxi's oldest daughter, Violet, who had long moved out and gotten married in 1921. Maxi's youngest daughter, Mabel, was already 27 years old and served as witness to the marriage so it seems unlikely that there was any bad blood.

Gladys and Philemon Buckley got married two years later, and raised their children, when they had them, in Spanish Town. Over the years, they lived at King Street, Manchester Street, Railway Lane and Walks Road. Gladys made a living doing laundry while Philemon worked as a carpenter.

The kids grew up and moved along. Some migrated and others moved to the big city, Kingston.

Gladys died of cancer when she was 61 years old. I felt a bit sad when I learned about that. I never knew her, but it seems that her life was so brief, and so difficult. Somehow it seems that by moving around so much, she was always eking out a living but never really got a chance to enjoy it as much as she perhaps should have. I probably read too much into all of this, but after looking at hundreds (maybe even thousands) of these birth, marriage and death certificates over the years, and reflecting on the fact that decades of their lives all come down to stringing a few pieces of paper together, I usually hope for some evidence of happiness and that they've left something of themselves behind. As I do when I am overwhelmed by the lives of family members of the past, I put down my research to clear my head for a day or two. It is all very sobering to relive their lives and think about how their decisions or heartbreaks make us who we are today. I admit to being an over-thinker, and I often think about whether my own life will be analyzed by some future generation of children or grandchildren as being futile or inconsequential.

Gilze-What?

I think the point in my research where I must have cross-checked every reference was when I came upon relatives by the surname "Gilzean."

As I mentioned earlier, Philemon Buckley was my father-in-law's dad. Philemon's mother was born Grace-Ann Buckley but had the maiden name Gilzean. Gilzean? I had never heard that name before! I wasn't even sure how it was pronounced. I was instantly fascinated. Unlike "Buckley", which had clear English origins and for which the common argument was easily made that a plantation owner simply gave his name to all his "property", something was telling me that this name had a story that might be a bit different. I began checking the origin of the name. "Gilzean" was Scottish; actually rather common in Scotland, in fact.

So who was Grace-Ann, and where was her family from? I found out that her father's name was Robert William Gilzean, the son of Alexander Gilzean Jr., who lived from about 1814 to 1884. Alexander was a first-generation Jamaican, you might call it. On the Slave Register of 1817, he was shown as a three-year-old mulatto (one black parent, one white parent), and was also known as "Alick". He and his 30-year-old mother Louisa were living on Expectation Hill estate, owned by one William Falconer in St. Mary, just over the St. Catherine border. St. Catherine was at the time known as St. Thomas in the Vale. Falconer's attorney was his cousin Alexander Gilzean (Senior) from Scotland.

Louisa's mother "Dilligence" was also living there among the 43 other enslaved people on that plantation. She was 70 years old and had been taken from Africa. Louisa had at least one other child with the surname Gilzean, namely, five-year-old Eliza, also known as Johanna. Her two eldest children, Amelia and Betsy, were not fathered by Gilzean. Amelia was listed as "Negro", and Betsy as "Sambo", meaning she had one negro parent and one mulatto parent. But what I really wanted to know was, was the relationship with Gilzean consensual or not?

Aside from being the attorney of Falconer's estate, Gilzean had a property of his own at the nearby plantation of Dunvegan in St. Thomas in the Vale. At Dunvegan, he had two boys who were given the names Thomas and James, born in 1811 and 1815, respectively. Their mother was an African woman named Sarah, who was about 19 or 20 when Thomas was born.

By 1820, Louisa, her mother, and all her children were now living on the Dunvegan estate. I located additional registers showing that she had been purchased by Alexander Gilzean, and had borne him two more children, namely James (who was born in 1816) and Thomas (born in 1818). I can only imagine how upsetting it was for each of them to have a half-brother with the same name!

Three years later in 1823, Louisa's mother Dilligence died, and so had nine-year-old Eliza. Louisa's son Allen, who was born around 1821, was not a Gilzean, based on the documentation of his race. It seems that her relationship with Alexander had come to an end. Who knows? Perhaps she had not realized until she moved to Dunvegan that there was another woman, and indeed, another family.

In 1832 things got really interesting. Alexander recorded the manumission (legal freedom) of Sarah's boys (Thomas and James) as well as Louisa's son Alexander. Two other children were also manumitted – Henrietta Kelly Gilzean and Isabella Gilzean. I found evidence that Isabella had been born to Sarah in 1828. The identity of Henrietta's mother is uncertain. What happened to Louisa's two other boys, Thomas and James? By 1832, they had been living on another property, belonging to Alexander's uncle and they too, were manumitted in that year.

Alexander Sr. returned to Scotland sometime after the abolition of the practice of slavery, and died in Banffshire in 1848 at the age of 71 years. There are records dating back many centuries naming Gilzeans, Kellys, and Gordons of Scotland and Ireland as predecessors of Alexander Gilzean, owner of Dunvegan plantation in Jamaica. Interestingly, Sarah's son Thomas also moved to Scotland and worked there as a tailor. He raised his family in Edinburgh and died of tuberculosis in 1868 at the age of 56.

Louisa's son Alexander remained in Jamaica and settled in Williamsfield, in the district of Harewood. His granddaughter Grace-Ann Gilzean later met William Buckley and they got married in 1890. Their son Philemon Buckley later became my husband's grandfather.

I admit that when all this information sank in, I was in disbelief. How could it be that I had managed to trace six generations of history which went back hundreds of years? In the case of the Gilzeans, in a matter of a few hours, I was able to locate additional stories which went all the way back into the 1400s and beyond. Remember, it was I who had frequently dismissed my daughter's urgings to embark on this project because I didn't want to get her hopes up, since she wouldn't understand that "our" world was different from "their" world. Granted, there are countless cultures which can trace back 10 or even 15 generations with relative ease, whereas it took me the better part of three years and lots of piecing together to find records for five or six generations. But when I think about the fact that I didn't expect to learn anything, well, I happen to find that pretty amazing and fulfilling.

The most glaring thing, however, was that the ones for whom I had extensive pieces of information were those who had been privileged to record — or to have recorded — their history. Even those Europeans who were uneducated, poor and less privileged knew exactly who they were. They had not been stripped of the stories and the memories of their fathers and mothers as others had been. I couldn't get away from the fact that the brick wall was definitely and undeniably linked to a deliberate attempt to erase the identity of an entire society – a cultural genocide, if you will.

How did my husband respond to this discovery? I think at first he didn't believe that my information could be trusted, but he started paying attention when I showed him a copy of his father's death certificate which I had found. Names of known family members who reported the death were there, the last place of residence which he knew to be factual, as well as other small details which he had never shared with me convinced him that I was doing real research and had found actual facts, not the usual anecdotes which accompany many Jamaican family stories.

When he heard about his great-grandmother's last name (Gilzean), he started paying attention. He was not acquainted with his paternal relatives and was now curious. However, as the story about his Scottish background began to take shape, I encountered emotions I was not altogether prepared for, namely anger and resentment. He was genuinely upset about how the union between a white Scot and an African or "Creole" was likely made, and he was not pleased. I suppose I should have expected this. He had often voiced strong opinions about colonizers legitimizing their own behaviour just because they put themselves in a position of authority. I have always been in a sort of passive agreement with him. Yes, there were times when I was momentarily fired up about it, but I was inconsistent at best and more than often dismissive about what could be done about it now.

However, with more details now available, a different picture began to emerge. Yes, Alexander had fathered multiple children with two women who were supposedly his "property", and the voices of these women have been so silenced that we cannot know with any certainty the true nature of the relationships. Even so, little clues such as the documents of manumission, the later emigration of one son, and most significantly, the provision of an inheritance to Sarah's children, suggest that at least their relationship was one of substance.

In his will, Alexander referred to Sarah as "Sarah Gilzean" even though there was no indication that they were officially married, and stated in the will that she was to be granted the use of a portion of the estate after his death for her lifetime. So, there it was. He viewed her as his wife. Louisa became "the other woman", I suppose, and her son, though bearing the same name as his father, was not mentioned in the will. His intention by granting his freedom was not to be overlooked though, and may have even indicated a relationship between father and son.

I often try to imagine what plantation life was really like in those days. Of course, in most ways I imagine it was very different when one compares transportation, communication and of course, authority. However, in some ways I think it may have been quite similar to today's Jamaica. For all Alexander's intentions, this type of behaviour normalized broken families and made survival a daily struggle. The ones who did survive were, by necessity, creative, strategic and resilient.

The Wilson Branch

The final branch of this tree belongs to my husband's maternal family. His maternal grandmother, Norma Wilson, died just a few years ago and I knew her quite well. The most curious thing happened when Sister Norma, as she was called, moved from Westmoreland to Kingston in the late 1970s. She lived at 26 Merrion Road for well over 20 years, directly across the street from 27 Merrion Road, where Philemon Buckley lived! This was unknown to everyone back in Westmoreland until years later when Aston's children slowly began moving to Kingston.

Looking back, we now believe that Sister Norma knew of the connection all along, but didn't want to get involved in what she perceived as family drama. Again, all families have characters and stories that you just can't make up. The truth is often stranger than fiction.

Sister Norma was the only child of Phillip Wilson ("Maas Phillip"), and Maud Rowe as a couple. Both of her parents had other children later, but Norma was the only product of that union. Anyway, one of Maud's other daughters later married someone by the name of Wilson who was, in fact, related to Norma.

My husband often jokes that he is related to some of his cousins on both sides of the family. It always confuses me, and he gets annoyed when I ask him to repeat the nature of the relationship, but I have since learned that this is more common than

I previously realized. The more common term is "double-cousins", and if you are true double-cousins, it means that instead of sharing about 12.5% of your DNA with that person as cousins usually do, you now share about 25% of your DNA. In this way, you are like half-siblings (genetically, of course).

Now initially, this was not of any direct interest to me, because my intention was never to go into great detail when researching cousins, but it did imply that some of the contradictions and unsolved mysteries I had come across with my earlier ancestors may be explained by this very same double-cousin phenomenon. There are people who have been identified as my second cousins once removed, or third cousins or some similar relationship because of our shared DNA, and with whom I have family surnames in common. However, sometimes we try to compare the names on our respective family trees and there are some contradictions because we may be equally sure of a great-grandparent's name, but they don't seem to match up. Well, knowing what I now know about community relationships in 1800s Jamaica, this is one possible explanation for not being able to connect the dots. So many families were formed within small communities which came out of plantation life. Therefore, there were bound to be situations where siblings chose their spouses from the same pool of families, and so the product of their unions were not just first cousins, but something closer. They would have had multiple common ancestors, so they shared more than the usual amounts of DNA. This has happened especially with my Boothe/Anglin relatives which I have found now, in the 21st century. Boothes and Anglins seem to have taken a liking to each other throughout the years and have made several unions. The result is that I now have a network of scores of relatives who are related to me through multiple distant relatives at various points in history. Isn't that something?

The Spencers

My husband learned recently that his maternal grandfather was named Samuel "Lemmy" Spencer.

I learned from another family member that Lemmy had worked at the wharf in Savanna-la-mar. This wharf would accommodate barges at the ramp mainly for sugar exports, but also for other cargo like rum, coconuts and logwood. Sugar trucks from the Frome Factory, about 20 minutes away, would bring in tons of the golden crystals to be sent all over the world. Until the 1960s, sugar production boomed. An agreement between Commonwealth countries like Jamaica and Britain ensured a market for the product and provided direct and indirect employment for thousands in Westmoreland and beyond.

Lemmy died of heart trouble in December 1960. His daughter was 12 years old and he was only 43. She never had any close connection to her paternal family. She has a vague recollection that he was originally from Darliston, but knows none of his family members. Spencer may have been the name of his father, or perhaps his mother, if they were unmarried. That is all we know.

The trickle-down result of all this is that my husband knew only one of his four grandparents. And since people don't like talking about aspects of their history that make them sad, uncomfortable or in any way upset, we have to tip-toe around many of our family members if we are to get much further.

I imagine that I will get further someday. I believe that the benefit of knowing more about our immediate and distant family members is slowly gaining momentum and acceptance, and that we will all learn from cultures which took care to write everything down so that they could learn from mistakes and build on the advances their parents made.

PART 2
REFLECTIONS

Lessons Learned

I once heard that education is not free. In order to learn, we must pay attention. That brilliantly sums up that I could have had one of two outcomes from embarking upon this project. It is easy to not pay attention, and only "learn" what I expected to, which was essentially nothing. But I tried as much as I could to pay attention to the education I was getting. It certainly wasn't free. It cost quite a bit of time, but also, I think, a sort of burden, to share a little of what I had learned by being more responsible in my speech and actions. Some of my formerly fuzzy or nuanced opinions are now quite clear to me, like my views on immigration, the idea of race, and the idea of language. These I will share, but again, they are not free. Pay attention.

Migration

I have always considered myself a practical sort of person, so on the subject of migration my personal views were usually formed by the stories depicted in movies or to a lesser extent, listening to personal experiences. I had always thought that the best place for me was home — the place where I grew up — and I was never an adventurous sort of person anyway. Think of me as the "tried-and-true" sort, as opposed to the "new-and-exciting".

When all my schoolmates had ideas of moving

to the United States when they were old enough, that idea literally never crossed my mind. Not only did I not have the desire to go, I wasn't even interested in knowing how one went about doing that. It just wasn't on my radar. As I grew older, maybe in my early 20s, I had co-workers who basically had that as their end goal. "Move to America. Make life better." But better than what? I had no major issues with my life, to be honest. I wasn't scratching for food; my immediate family was right where I wanted them and I enjoyed the predictability of having a general idea of what next year would look like.

In fact, that's what I told my husband when the idea of moving to Canada came up in my late 20s. Why would we want to leave? And to be immigrants? (It really did seem like a dirty word.) I thought about all those movies I saw where people were all crammed in the city in some dingy apartment building, hustling for low-paying jobs, hiding from the authorities and dreaming of that elusive day they would return home wealthy, but the audience knew that it would never happen. We explored the idea briefly, but I really wasn't up to it and I convinced him at the time that it wasn't a good idea.

But you know how it is when you have an itch. I think he had the itch. He wanted to do something different, see someplace else, experience what others had. While I couldn't personally relate to those feelings, I now know that they do exist for many, many people. I have had friends who shared with me that they wouldn't mind experiencing a different, unknown problem (or job) just so that they wouldn't have to deal with their current problem (or job). To me, that's crazy talk, but enough people have expressed that for me to know that it isn't a far-fetched notion.

So he had the itch. And sure enough, the idea came up again a few years later. This time, I thought to myself, "If you had a dream and the one thing holding you back is this person you hitched yourself to years ago, you would resent them forever, especially since they could give you no valid reason for denying that dream." So we took the leap and left Jamaica.

It was everything I thought it would be, and then some. There were many times I regretted leaving the stability and privileges that came with being on familiar ground. But I also experienced something I hadn't banked on: a real-life education in the subjects of society, employment, language, culture, psychology and self, which I previously hadn't thought I was deficient in.

This book has been a part of that education. I knew what I wanted to find when I started the journey. But I learned so much more. I am happy that I got to meet my foreparents of 200 years ago, and that I learned things from their lives which make me humbler about my own life. I learned about relationships and that families are still doing what they have always done to survive and to make life better for the generations that haven't been born yet. I learned about difficult decisions which have to be made, and that one way or the other, you don't know whether it's the right one but it can and will affect those who come after you, for better or worse.

I learned about people who were not my ancestors, but with whom I do share my Jamaican identity, groups like the East Indian, Chinese, Middle Eastern and poor European migrants to the Caribbean. Many of them came voluntarily, much like my migration to Canada, perhaps wanting a better life for themselves, but really thinking of a better life for their children. I learned about changes to government policy (or sometimes just plain old shenanigans) which caused people to be stuck thousands of miles away from home, sometimes worse off than before, with little chance of returning. I learned that the individuals who didn't roll over and play dead had the best fighting chance to make it over the next hurdle which was sure to come along.

While learning about my ancestors' lives for the past few years, I just haven't been able to get this line of a song I used to hear while growing up in Jamaica in the 1980s out of my head. The song, "Solidarity," recorded by Black Uhuru, speaks about the universality of people's wants. We all want essentially the same things for ourselves and our families, even though we may go about achieving them in different ways.

That just about sums up why people have migrated for thousands of years. There is nothing in this that is unique to Jamaican, American, Jewish, British, Viking, Italian, Syrian or any other people. Everybody wants the same thing. Don't they?

"It Never Happened"

One evening, in my excitement about this project, I shared with a couple who were friends of ours the discoveries I was making about our history, slavery and the like. We like this couple very much and the husband could easily be considered my husband's best friend. He gave a kind of quiet laugh and said to me, "You are going to be surprised when I tell you what I think of all of this."

I figured he was going to be the usual Doubting Thomas about the genuineness of the records I found. I could deal with that. "Okay; well, what do you think?" I asked.

He laughed nervously. "I don't think any such thing happened. I don't believe slavery existed."

Words cannot describe the confusion I felt. Was he just making a joke? No, I looked him straight in the eyes and he was quite serious, albeit a little dismissive. He then explained to me that he believed that the entire history we have been taught about the Transatlantic Slave Trade was a hoax, exaggerated stories told and retold for the sake of sensationalism.

"So how," I asked, "did so many people of African origin end up on this side of the world?"

"Natural migration," he shrugged.

Well, my mind was blown. I could not comprehend that such a close friend, with whom I grew up, was denying the existence of the most accepted 400 years of my — our — ancestors' history. I was no longer feeling confused, but instead hurt and angry. I was stammering, making reference to calls for reparations for slavery. Surely, I reasoned with him, the colonizers would have quickly shot down any such request by simply pointing out that no such slave trade had ever existed. He defended his position by stating that slavery stories were great for tourism, and the stories had already gotten out of hand, more or less, so they all had to just go with it.

"But what about all the documentary evidence?" I argued, not believing what I was hearing.

"Falsified."

"Did you know about this?" I asked his wife accusingly.

"No," she laughed, shrugged and looked almost as surprised as I was.

I was so upset at what I was hearing that I couldn't say any more on the topic. I changed the subject and tried to remain in a good mood for the rest of the evening.

A year later this episode was still bugging me. How to explain it? I deconstructed it the following way:

How does knowledge of the Transatlantic Slave Trade make me feel? Initially, indifferent. I accept it as a fact and overall it didn't affect my view of the British, other Europeans or the Africans who contributed to it. But when I "met" my grandparents from five, six or seven generations ago and got to discover their sad lives, the multiple children they lost at an early age from preventable sicknesses due to poverty or lack of education, the inability to sign their own names on a legal document because they could neither read nor write and the splitting up of families to try to make life better elsewhere, I now understood the emotion. Yes, it was anger, but it sprung from a feeling of injustice.

Why had my forefathers been the unfortunate ones, treated as cattle and then made to live lives of desperation and unhappiness? Why, at the abolition of slavery, did they have to start from scratch, driven mainly by their own desire to improve their lot in a system designed to make others profit through their suffering?

I imagine that everyone who starts their own family project secretly fantasizes that they will discover some famous relative, some influential family member to make them feel proud, make them able to boast to their friends, "Oh, did you know that my grandfather's father was so-and-so?" Instead, my research had brought me face-to-face with the reality of most of us of Caribbean birth: most of my forebears were children of enslaved people and victims of oppression. I felt hurt and helpless, unable to do anything about it. And that, I believe, hit the nail on the head.

My theory is that my friend who denies institutionalized slavery may not want to think that relatively few generations ago, his ancestors were tortured, beaten, enslaved, raped or humiliated in some other way. In short, he responds by denying it ever happened. It's an extreme response, of course, but it now makes perfect sense to me. In a way, it's more effective than the classic anger response in that it allows you to live a peaceful life without being angry at the offender. Viewed from that perspective, I forgive him. Everyone has their coping mechanism and I may have discovered a new one. I wonder how many other people of African descent have responded in this way.

My problem with this particular coping strategy is that it stops short of acknowledging that starting with next to nothing, our fathers and mothers did what they could to make improvements for each successive generation even if they couldn't do so for themselves. From slavery to apprenticeship to paid employment, property and business ownership, education and creativity, we are standing on the building blocks which were laid by our very determined, hard-working and resourceful predecessors.

"Slaves"

I have come to take exception to the use of the

word "slaves" with reference to people of African descent who were forcibly taken to the Americas. Now before you start eye-rolling about me not accepting the past as the past, just hear me out and if you don't agree, then so be it and there is no love lost. The Oxford Dictionary says that a slave is as a person who is the legal property of another and is forced to obey them. I'm focusing here on the word "legal". Well, slavery ended in England around the 1100s and was replaced by serfdom, which looked suspiciously similar to the apprenticeship which was enforced in Jamaica after "emancipation". But that's another story for another book, maybe.

Anyway, centuries before the Transatlantic Slave Trade, the British decided that they would no longer taint their land with such an uncivilized practice as shackling and whipping fellow human beings into servitude. There were even a few cases where Englishmen "purchased" Africans, brought them back to England, and this resulted in general confusion, since this was socially and otherwise unacceptable.

Despite the practice of slavery being well-known and accepted in British colonies, as early as the 18th century there were court rulings which indicated that:

"by the common law no man can have property in another," *(Holt CJ, Smith vs. Gould, 1705-07)*

and

"as soon as a man sets foot on English ground he is free" *(Lord Henley LC, Shanley v. Harvey, 1763)*

This was, in fact, while British citizens openly made their wealth enslaving humans in foreign countries while their own families lived in splendour and grandeur at home. The point is, if the English knew that there was no legal provision for slavery in their own country, on what basis did they seek to enslave Africans (or anyone else, for that matter) in their colonies overseas?

The use of the word "slave" was an attempt at legitimizing a set of activities which was less than legitimate. The plain truth is that human trafficking was big business. Millions of people were kidnapped and transported against their will and then made to work under penalty of death. The fact that forced labour was no longer practised in England confirms that there was a consciousness that it was morally wrong. This explains why it was only conveniently practised thousands of miles away from the finery and grandeur which it financed. By such reasoning, no one had any right to claim that these men and women who had been forcibly taken from their homes were the "legal" property of anyone, as this act would not even have been allowed in the land of the colonizers.

I know there will be the argument that slavery existed in Africa, but this too was very different from the chattel slavery introduced in the Caribbean and America. Someone in Africa might be "enslaved" to work off a debt, or if he had committed a crime (similar to today's practice of putting someone in prison, I guess). There was usually a provision whereby the slave would later become free. Chattel slavery, on the other hand, stipulated that a slave had no rights, was a slave for life, and his or her children and grandchildren were likewise property of the "master".

I challenge this practice on the basis that there was no precedence for this practice in any of the lands where the deeds were committed, that is to say, there was no "legality" of the action, because the act of stealing someone from their home and forcibly transporting them to a foreign country was not recognized, neither in the African territories from which they were stolen, nor in the lands to which they were transported. To make matters worse, slavery was not allowed in the land of the slave traders either! Some of these people who were illegally and forcibly taken were prominent members of their communities, family men and women, parents, teenagers who went out for a regular day and never made it back because they were kidnapped by or for strangers who wanted free labour to enrich themselves.

Of course, this entire wretched business was only possible because there were neighbors who were ready and willing to capitalize on this demand in exchange for the promise of wealth. I don't deny this. But my point is, all of this was done surreptitiously. This was not the natural order of things. It was all new, uncharted territory and set in motion a new normal for billions of people for hundreds of years.

So I believe the more accurate term is "enslaved people", rather than "slaves", making the point that they were not in fact, the legal property of anyone, but an illegal claim had been laid upon them which could not be justified, even by the prevailing practice of the day. It was only made legal in lands where, having decimated the previous population, the beneficiaries of this scheme were now free to make new rules.

Yes, it's a mouthful, I know, but I feel the need to clearly state my point so I am not accused of being petty or trifling. Words are important and I made the point earlier that there is a feeling of shame at being a descendant of generations of slaves. Of course, there is really nothing to be ashamed of, much like a rape victim has no real reason to feel that they did anything wrong, but the fact is that they do feel that way. The act of violence and moral injustice was done against them, but like rape, being enslaved was such an invasion of one's person that it created a shame that made the victim look upon themselves negatively.

I suppose a psychologist could better explain why this happens only with some kinds of acts and not others, but I am not trying to dissect the psychology of it. I'm just saying that in the same way that the usage of other words has changed with the passing of time due to offensive connotations, maybe it's time to start looking at this word "slave" in this particular context, and teach ourselves to use the more accurate term "enslaved people", or some other expression which better conveys who these people were and what was done to them. The shame should go back to the perpetrators, not the victims.

Race and Colour

I've also become a little annoyed by the use of the word "race". A member of a Facebook group once asked members what race we each considered ourselves, namely Black, Mixed, or something else. He definitely was not prepared for the answers that came his way. My personal response was that I don't even understand what the word means. It seems to be a system of classification that isn't real, and certainly isn't useful. I can understand people being grouped based on where they live or were born, hence "nationality", or even their ethnicity (e.g. "Caribbean"), but I simply don't see any merit in grouping people based on how they look. You will not learn anything meaningful about me by deciding if I am "Black" or "White". It isn't accurate, because people can and do come to all sorts of conclusions which are often wrong one way or the other.

For example, if someone whom you have known for 20 years and whom you assumed to be Caucasian suddenly revealed to you that they were in fact not Caucasian, would that revelation change anything you already knew about them? It wouldn't. What if that same person revealed that they were raised in Japan? You would now understand their love for a certain type of music, art or food.

The very idea of choosing the words "Black" or "White" seems flawed and a bit suspicious, since human beings do not bear those colours anyway. It seems to me that the selection of those particular colours was a deliberate attempt to paint a picture of two sets of people who are as different from each other as possible. Granted, it isn't my job to tell others how to refer to themselves, but I usually just refer to myself as Jamaican – not Black, Mixed-race, nor anything similar. I don't get offended if others do, however, because I realize that not everyone shares my view, or has even thought about the subject at all. And then there are those who have thought of it, but there are few useful alternative words, so they stick to the terms we're used to. I understand that, and accept why our language may be deficient, cumbersome and problematic in this regard.

I also accept that describing a person by the shade of their skin simply to distinguish one from the other may be useful in certain circumstances. This is commonly practiced in Jamaica where people are referred to as "black/dark-skinned", "brown" or "white", referring solely to the physical skin tone. However, in the wider world, and specifically in North America, there is a phenomenon whereby people do not refer to people of African descent as "brown" regardless of their skin-tone. No matter the shade of skin, that person is "Black". And no matter the shade of a Caucasian person's skin, they are simply "White". A person of Indian descent is always "Brown", regardless of how dark or pale their skin is. This practice confirms my conclusion that these colours are simply a system of classification that serves to reinforce outdated ideas of hierarchy, whether deliberate or not.

PART 3
THE MAP

Your Journey

Tip 1 – What Do You Want to Know?

As I mentioned in "What Are You Looking For?" in the My Journey section, what started as a simple desire to build a four-generation family tree became a three-year quest resulting in discovering the names and stories of over 500 family members and a much richer and accurate idea of the legacy of my ancestors. My mission changed as I went along, of course, but at least I had some kind of target to guide where my research was going.

You may have a different purpose for your research. Maybe you're trying to find out about a parent you don't know too much (or anything) about. Maybe someone migrated and you're trying to track down what happened to them. Or maybe you're just curious about what you can find. Whatever the case, your perspective will probably change as you get to know more about the personal details of your family members.

The point is, if you don't have any questions, you can't get them answered. It's that simple. You can always revise or refine the questions later, but definitely write them down and start there! It can be one question which later branches off into two or three smaller ones. Or it could be multiple questions. Whatever the case, don't worry; they will ask themselves as you start finding family members and mysteries to solve.

Tip 2 - Identify the Storytellers

You know the storytellers in your family. They are disguised as the aunt who knows everyone's business, the nosy cousin, or the long-winded older relative who everybody avoids asking questions because the answer is always too long and never quite what you were hoping for. I started by talking to my parents about the project and my dad, who is the storyteller in my family, was instantly excited. He named the people he most wanted more information about: his grandparents. He told me the names of their parents based on what he had heard them repeat while growing up.

My mother was more contained in her enthusiasm but she named a family member whom she had been trying to trace for years, a cousin from whom we had gained family land but lost contact with after she migrated to Panama in the early 20th century. My mother reminded me of her grandmother's name (she didn't have to; my siblings and I felt like we knew her because our childhood was punctuated by stories of Mabel Drummond), but she couldn't give me the names of her grandmother's parents, so I felt, "Okay, this is going to be a very short branch of the tree." There were also some anecdotes which my parents wanted to either confirm or rule out: our reported relation to two well-known Jamaican political figures – Sir Alexander Bustamante (formerly Clarke) on my father's side, and Osmond Theodore (O.T.) Fairclough on my mother's side. They asked me to check that out if I could.

During my months of research, I searched for more family stories. My immediate family members live in various locations and they couldn't seem to understand how much their little stories interested me. All except my dad. He is always willing and ready to go down memory lane, with anyone who will listen. The gamble is that I may not get a story about what I'm asking for. It's kind of funny, actually. I will ask about Old Joe and end up hearing the history of Old Joe's cat, or his horse, or his one-legged handyman. But it's all good. One thing is certain: my dad's stories are never boring – they just tend to take you a bit left of what you're actually looking for.

Whether they are natural storytellers or not, the oldest members of your family or in your community represent a portion of history which cannot be replaced after they are gone. Of course, documents and facts will still be there, but their feelings and opinions are unique to them and will be gone if not captured in some way. But don't just reach out to them for the specific questions that you want answered – really listen to them, and take down as much detail as you can. Maybe you will find something you never knew you were looking for. In these days when video recordings can be done inexpensively by cell phones, and can be duplicated, distributed and saved "to the cloud" so that the data isn't lost when the device is lost or destroyed, you may want to consider storing voice and video interviews for yourself and later generations to look back on.

Tip 3 – Get Organized

There are two ways to organize the information you have collected: manually and electronically. I do both.

Manual Organization

Unlike my original choice of a notebook, I strongly recommend that you use a binder. That way, as you get to meet more relatives from the past, as you most definitely will, you can add names without affecting the flow or organization of your work too much. Aside from that, I liked the system of organization I chose. My notebook had no built-in dividers, so I bought Post-It strips and used them to create tabs so that I could effortlessly jump to the family name I wanted. At first, I divided my book into three major surnames. I assumed (correctly) that I would later need to add more last names, and I wouldn't need that many pages for each name anyway.

I later realized that it was quite convenient that I could insert tabs as needed later on when I stumbled upon family names that I hadn't known about before. This would happen because I naturally discovered names which were useful to the stories I was telling, and would create branches of their own. It therefore made sense to me to keep certain last names closer to each other, rather than just organizing them alphabetically.

For example, I later inserted Gilzean as a sub-tab behind Buckley, because the Buckleys in our family descended from the Gilzeans. Similarly, I created Boothe as sub-tab behind Fairclough, because though my mom's last name was Fairclough, I discovered that she descended from Boothes and Anglins, which were major last names in their own right in the history of our family and in the area where they settled.

This is why a binder is an infinitely better idea than a notebook. That way, you can easily remove, insert or move pages around as necessary. I allocated about 10 pages for each last name. I started with the surnames I was most curious about – names based on the questions I asked in Tip 1. The tabs I created initially were:

1. Fairclough (my mom's maiden name)
2. Clarke (my dad's surname)
3. Buckley (my husband's surname)

The tabs became like easy-to-jump-to chapter names, and each fact I learned was converted into a one-line bullet point below a character's name. I would use these facts as my starting points for asking more questions, or for doing additional research later. These would serve as important points of reference to keep me grounded when I got stuck or lost focus.

Electronic Organization

At some point, however, you will run out of pages, and at any rate, it would be a tragedy to do hours, weeks or months of research and get it wet, burnt or simply lost. For this reason, nothing beats saving your research electronically. Some people invest in different types of genealogical software, which are (honestly speaking) amazing tools of organization and which offer excellent graphical representations of family data. Naturally however, genealogical software is not free and often not even cheap. At any rate, I promised to share family research tips on a budget, and below are some suggestions.

If you are on a shoestring budget, you will definitely want to know about familysearch.org. This is a free, not-for-profit website which holds digitized copies of millions of birth, marriage and death (BMD) records as well as census records, military documents and the like. You can create a family tree with an unlimited number of names, and attach the source documents you have located. However, this is by no means the only, nor – some may argue – the best online research tool available.

One major drawback with familysearch.org is that it is considered a community website. The only names on your tree which are private are individuals who are documented as still living. Community ownership also means that people are free to add and delete names on your tree. It rarely happens, and people don't do it out of spite, but if an enthusiastic researcher who isn't as savvy as you are gets loose on your tree – look out. You may lose valuable hours and years of research if you don't have it recorded elsewhere. That being said, I only had two instances of someone incorrectly amending names and details of my family members on familysearch.org. I reached out to them, explaining why my details were correct, and they apologized. This is usually the response, and I've continued to use the site because it serves my purpose. You should take the time to determine what is right for you based on your needs and the pros and cons of each resource. Refer to Appendix III – Resources Cheat Sheet for my personal shortlist.

Tip 4 – Set Aside Some Time

I can guarantee you one thing – you won't find the time to do all the homework required to do this project the way you want to. Let's face it – no one has copious amounts of time just lying around, waiting for your next big project to fill the gaps. Whether you work part-time, full-time or double-time. Whether you work from home or you're unemployed. Whether you're a student, single, married or none of the above – you will never find enough time to do this properly. Nope. You will have to make the time.

Get up half an hour earlier, go to bed half an hour later. Watch less TV, or get your family members to share chores. Speaking of family members, if they are as excited as you are about this undertaking of yours, great. But don't be surprised if your enthusiasm is met with confusion or annoyance. Not everyone will understand why you are pouring energy into something that is not financially profitable or at least "practical". This may even cause you to start feeling a bit guilty. Don't.

I'm not saying you should neglect your family or your responsibilities, but a good way to think of it is to treat it as you would a hobby. Some people play a sport, some read books and some go to the gym. You research your family history. I recommend treating it with the same priority as you would any other hobby. Maybe you do it once a week. One thing is certain: it definitely helps if your family is on board. So, like I said, try to get their cooperation. Use the same reasoning. "This is my hobby; it helps me relax." That worked for me, and I imagine, will be a reasonable argument for most people. If not, then I recommend coming to some agreement in order to reduce family friction as much as possible. Wait until they are engaging in their hobbies, or reduce your research blocks to 30 minutes at a time. It makes no sense to learn about your dead family members by alienating the living ones.

Be aware that this hobby can go on forever. Despite having specific questions that you set out to answer, the nature of this type of research is such that the more you find out, the more questions you will ask. Therefore, if your ultimate goal is to write a book, or to create a family tree, or some other specific target, you may want to write that down so that you'll know when you get there.

For example, if you want to trace four generations of ancestors on both sides of your family tree, that means you've reached your goal when you have 30 names of direct ancestors (your two parents, your four grandparents, your eight great-grandparents, and your 16 great-grandparents). At that point, you can re-evaluate if you want to continue with a new target or not. But suppose you were doing this to present a chart for a family gathering, or some other time-sensitive event; you run the risk of getting sidetracked by some interesting story along the way and not reaching your target. And I promise you – there will be lots to get you sidetracked.

Along the way, I found my discoveries so engrossing and my searches so addictive that, despite my tendency to be risk-averse, I signed up for products, services and membership on sites (mostly free) which I would have turned my nose up at prior to embarking on this journey. You will also call and email strangers to piece puzzles together. I stayed up until the wee hours of the morning while I chipped away at some frustrating mystery until I was satisfied that I had found the answer.

Tip 5 – Don't Depend on Just the Stories

After talking to the storytellers and the older members of your family, you will soon realize that you have gone back 100 years, maximum. And that is a very generous number. More likely, you will get 70-80 years of good, solid memories. Beyond that you are likely getting a vague patchwork of contradictory family lore and legend that no one seems able to verify and that sometimes sounds suspect anyway.

Your family members may either be convinced about their own stories or they may sound doubtful, but that is usually a function of their own personalities. Getting someone else in the family to verify may not be any more reliable because both stories may have originated from the same source. At this point it becomes pretty obvious that you need to find:

i. primary sources, and
ii. independent sources

A primary source is one which records an event at or shortly after the occurrence of the event. As a rule, when an event is documented long after it took place, that document tends to be less accurate than one which was recorded in the moment or shortly thereafter. This is why the date of birth on one's birth certificate is more likely to be accurate than the date of birth on one's death certificate. Of course, this doesn't mean that there haven't been cases where the reverse took place, but this is out of the norm and the rule of thumb usually works. This is also why the storytellers in your family, fascinating as their stories may be, are considered secondary sources if they are retelling the story to you just now. Some old-timers are notorious for embellishing facts, while others may simply not remember the details as well as they believe they do. I struck gold when I found the diary of Philemon Buckley's World War I military commander, which recorded daily activities and events of his battalion. This is an example of a primary source.

An independent source is one which is not connected to your first source. The more independent sources you have, the more credible your story is. Examples of independent sources may be newspapers, government documents or even eyewitness accounts. An independent source may be primary or secondary.

You will almost certainly be surprised at the number of people with the same first and last names. This was mainly because many people living on a plantation ended up taking the same last names even after emancipation, and were basically using the same "pool" of colonial first names: Mary, Elizabeth, Alexander, William and so on. There was little creativity, since most of the population was unable to read and write, so I suppose there was the thought that these were the "proper" names to give to a child. Quite often, I would locate a record that looked like the one I needed, but could not be absolutely certain it referred to the family member I was looking for. I would therefore often use what I later discovered was called the FAN (family, associates and neighbours) technique – looking up information about siblings, friends and other community members and tying that in to what you already know, then working backwards to get the information you truly want. As you can imagine, this can be quite tedious, but is extremely useful and has the additional benefit of helping to piece stories together.

You may also find that you have a family member who was also interested in preserving history. They may not have had the resources which are available to us today, but their interest and earlier legwork may save you some time. Realize that you may have to think outside of the box a bit. For instance, here is a tip I'm happy to share:

After reaching a plateau in my research (I had found direct ancestors as far as seven generations back, and was now only making lateral discoveries, like aunts, cousins and the like), I was visiting my parents and thought to myself that I should make copies of my grandparents' photos, which my mom had. Then it clicked. My mom has been keeping funeral programs as well as wedding invitations and programs for years. As you may already know, weddings and funerals are a huge deal in Jamaica. This may be surprising to more conservative cultures, but the cost of an average Jamaican funeral may run around the same as a very lavish wedding.

Firstly, funeral homes make a killing (pardon the pun) because the body is often stored until relatives from overseas can get the time off from work to attend. It is not unheard of to have bodies stored for three to four weeks while funeral arrangements are made. Aside from obtaining the best-looking coffin one can (or cannot) afford, there is the whole matter of providing food for crowds of visitors for usually nine nights after the death, sometimes hiring the services of a deejay to make everyone feel merry, making sure there is an abundance of liquor freely available. A friend of mine revealed that grave-digging is a whole-day event that often involves a deejay and copious amounts of liquor and food. And of course the real party is the evening of the burial itself, where everything mentioned before takes place but is twice as lavish. The family is expected to provide at least a curried goat (a Jamaican delicacy and by no means cheap). The entire community turns up for this whosoever-will-may-come party, so there had better be enough food and drink to feed an army if your loved one was popular.

Another often-overlooked, but relatively pricey expense is the funeral program. Yes, that simple document which functions simply to list the name, birth and death dates of the deceased, order of the service and maybe a short blurb on their life accomplishments, is often so chock-full of useful information to an amateur genealogist, that it should definitely be sought out. You will most likely find detailed life summaries and timelines, as well as full-colour pictures of cousins, siblings and the deceased's milestones over the years. In my mom's keepsake drawer, I found 103 funeral programs neatly locked away, several of which were quite useful in establishing or clarifying relationships about which I had been uncertain or unaware.

There is also the question of whether to DNA-test or not. There seems to be the idea that a DNA test will tell you everything you need to know about who you are. This is simply not true. In fact, doing DNA-testing opens up a whole new set of questions, with new concepts to understand. Besides, it's not very accurate in determining specific locations, and it doesn't claim to be. It can't tell you for certain which tribe or even which country in the continent of Africa or Europe or Asia your people came from. It does give you a general idea of where in the world the majority of your ancestors may have been as far as eight generations back. With that information, you can connect with people who are related to you by DNA and figure out who your common ancestors are.

Just because it is fashionable doesn't mean you should do it. There are many ethical questions which people have started asking, like: How will my data be used? Can it be used against me later by my health insurance company? Should I give permission for law enforcement to take action against someone who is established as my family member on the basis of my DNA? What about sending in samples for people who are unable to give legal consent, such as children or elderly relatives with diminished mental capacity? Make sure that you decide on the answers to these and similar questions before you are clear on how you will proceed.

I did the test. It was mostly out of curiosity, but I did not give any additional permissions (for storage, or any other use) because I'm more of a private person. I've also refused to allow my daughter to be tested at this time. She is still underage and it's too big of a decision to make for her, considering it's something that is not absolutely necessary.

Tip 6 – Set Aside Some Money

I make no claim to be able to teach you how to do worthwhile family research without spending some money. I went close to one year collecting and documenting without spending a penny on this project. And I got pretty far, too. I went back about four generations and had a respectable number of names on my family tree (about 50-65, including cousins). But I realized that the juicy stuff – the stories, the whys and hows – weren't going to come for free.

I am frugal by nature. Or maybe by nurture. My mother, an accountant by profession, got us all on board saving money while growing up. I love saving money. I will save it just to see it sitting there and I won't even take credit to say that it's because I am so disciplined; I just hate to spend money. When I spend a dollar, you can be sure that it had to be spent.

And I'll tell you something else – it was worse before I got married. Mind you, I never saw this as a problem. Not until I observed and secretly admired the liberal financial philosophies of my husband. Phrases like, "What are we working for?" "Who is going to spend my money when I die?" and, "If I wait till I'm rich, I will never spend" shocked, scared and fascinated me all at once. I still consider myself the more financially responsible of us both (that can stay between you and me), but I am grateful that I have become kinder and more "human" as a result of seeing things from another point of view. Knowing my husband has caused me to help others even when I myself am in need, and to worry less than I used to about where my next penny will come from.

That said, I'm still not cured. I deliberate, hesitate and procrastinate when it's time to part with my money. But there was no getting around it: DNA and family research are incredibly fashionable right now and though it took me months to reach into my wallet and pay for a DNA test from one of those online companies, I did it. And, as with most of my purchases, I didn't regret it.

There were many testing companies available, the most popular ones being Ancestry, 23andme, MyHeritage and Family Tree DNA. I only seriously considered Ancestry and 23andme since those two had the largest customer bases and heavily advertise on this side of the globe. MyHeritage has a large base of European customers, and Family Tree DNA has a wide representation of ethnicities but a smaller customer base. I therefore reasoned that I would statistically get more matches from one of the first two websites. I finally decided to go with 23andme, the main reason being that a work colleague of mine had done hers and posted her ethnicity results online, and I just liked the layout of it. I hadn't seen any samples of what the Ancestry ones looked like, but I liked the friendliness and ease of use of the 23andme website so they got my money. I also think that Ancestry's constant TV commercials turned me off somehow (yes, I hate to think that a commercial has "worked" on me, so I usually go with the less aggressive marketer).

Truth be told, if you are considering purchasing one of these kits, I think both companies are equal in terms of their reliability and will likely give you similar results. I am acquainted with many genealogists, both serious and amateur, who have tested using one or the other (and some, both) with no major complaints or preference as it relates to both companies' DNA testing platform. One advantage of Ancestry is that they also offer access to documents (for a separate fee, of course). And since their database of users is larger, you have access to more family trees, which means more clues. Several of these documents are available for free on familysearch.org, but without the trees of other users, sometimes you are just stuck. I managed without an Ancestry membership for three years, until I decided to take them up on a special offer of three months for $1. I couldn't pass up a deal like that, and I must admit that I found new information much more quickly than I would have on my own. The point though, is this: you will have to set some money aside if you want to find out more than just names.

Understand that the kit you will likely purchase is your own (at first). As you start matching with strangers who are your second, third or third cousins twice removed, you will naturally want to find out how you are related – on your maternal, or your paternal side? And who was the common ancestor? What was the story? One way to find this out is to test another member of your family. Here is a little hack you can bear in mind: half-siblings are good for eliminating some of the guess-work in determining the answers to questions like those.

As you ask your relatives for their permission to test their DNA online, naturally you will be the one to pay for these kits. Nevertheless, be sure to explain to your relative(s) the implications of what you are doing. Also prepare them for unexpected results. I have seen so many cases of families being disrupted because of paternity secrets or other secrets being revealed this way. There is also the real possibility that law enforcement may use your DNA to find a criminal simply by looking at close matches. For example, if the DNA left at a crime scene is a 50% match with one on an online database, it's pretty easy to narrow down the owner of the crime scene DNA. It has to be a very close family member (such as a sibling or parent, etc.) That's how law enforcement solved several 40-year old cases by arresting the Golden State serial killer in 2018.

Here is another tip: in celebration of families, testing companies often offer kit discounts around family-themed holidays, so it pays to wait around and look out for these.

You may also end up spending money traveling to some of the locations where your family members lived. I was quite prepared to do this until I discovered that I could do so virtually for free. Google Earth offers a 3D representation of locations, and allows you to create projects where you can map places so as to understand and visualize the relative locations between places. You can also measure distances, add or view landmarks and save all these actions for reference later.

Think, too, of all the phone calls to family members overseas. Now, if you have WhatsApp, Skype or a similar Voice over IP phone, great. But some family members, depending on their level of tech-readiness or their geographic location, may not have access to, or know how to use, the internet. Whatever the case, take note of your personal circumstances and budget accordingly.

I took advantage of a free one-month subscription to newspaperarchive.com and was delighted to find numerous articles which gave tidbits of information about my relatives and offered great insight into their daily lives. For each free trial subscription, be sure to set a reminder for three to five days prior to the expiry date to prompt you to discontinue the subscription so that you are not automatically charged for renewal.

Tip 7 – Network with Like-Minded Folks

At some point in your research (likely several times), you will hit a roadblock. You run out of ideas for locating an ancestor, or you come across a record that is illegible or ambiguous, or you just need an explanation for some seeming contradiction. That's where crowdsourcing is extremely useful.

You may already know this, but there is a Facebook (FB) group for practically everything. A FB group for people who love cats, a FB group for volunteers who meet to clean toilets and a FB group to discuss things you can accomplish before the microwave reaches 0:00. It should come as no surprise, then, that there are groups of people just like you who are interested in finding out more about their family's history. There are so many groups in fact, that you may have trouble deciding which one(s) to join. You can join as many as you like. They usually ask a few qualifying questions to ensure that you're in the right place, and that you understand the rules of membership.

Once you're in, take a look around so you get a feel of the mood of the group. Importantly, read the announcements they usually have pinned to the top for new members. It may answer frequently asked questions or have resources for exactly what you're looking for, or for things you didn't even know you could or should look for.

Another useful feature in FB groups is a small section in the left panel that says "Search this group". Here, you can enter a word or phrase that you are researching and if it has been mentioned in the group before, all those posts will show up in the main section. This may be a last name, a location or something unique that you believe you may share with other family members.

The Admins of these genealogy research groups are also great resources. They are usually serious (albeit mostly amateur) genealogists who devote their personal time and years' worth of manned hours into understanding how genealogy works. They have a great deal of experience and can offer tips and tricks that will save you a ton of time and effort. Since they are not often engaged in this for professional reasons, they are usually happy to help you do a little detective work for free, or to understand a record you found. Bear in mind that they are still just people, and some are more helpful than others. The memberships of these groups often overlap and you will see several of the same members appearing in more than one group.

These groups are also great ways of finding out when something interesting or useful is happening in the family research universe. It was a post from a member which told me about the $1 subscription to Ancestry which gave me three months of full access to records and other family trees which were gold in uncovering questions I had. It was also a FB group member who shared that newspaperarchives.com was offering a free one-month access to newspapers dating back to the year 1607.

There are other ways to network too. There are genealogical societies, podcasts, newsletters and prestigious universities which offer free short courses in doing this type of research. Government bodies, like the Registrar General's Department of Jamaica, offer genealogical research for a nominal fee by visiting their website and filling out an application form. Your own local library may have an expert who comes in once a month or at some other interval to help folks like yourself. In short, there is no shortage of help, and therefore no excuse for not getting started.

REFERENCES

Alexis, Simone. 2012. *Re: Clark Clarke St Ann Jamaica.* 05 23. https://www.genealogy.com/forum/regional/countries/topics/jamaica/6986/.

Bennett, Hazel, and Phillip M. Sherlock. 1998. *The Story of the Jamaican People.* Ian Randle Publishers.

Blackburn, Robin. 1988. The Overthrow of Colonial Slavery: 1776-1848. London: Verso.

Dickson, Arthur Richard. 2005. "A snapshot of people and life in Lucea & Hanover, circa 1913 – 1933." *Lucea Online.* http://www.lucea-online.com/Lucea1920-1933inc.PicDec05.pdf.

Editorial, Caribbean National Weekly. 2019. "Paternity Predicament: More Jamaican Men Are Getting "Jackets"." *Caribbean National Weekly*, November 1.

Grannum, Guy. 2011. "Researching African-Caribbean Family History." *British Broadcasting Corporation.* February 17. http://www.bbc.co.uk/history/familyhistory/next_steps/genealogy_article_01.shtml.

Hesman Saey, Tina. 2018. "DNA testing can bring families together, but gives mixed answers on ethnicity." *ScienceNews*, June 13.

Imperial War Museums. n.d. "The Story Of The British West Indies Regiment In The First World War." Accessed April 2020. https://www.iwm.org.uk/history/the-story-of-the-british-west-indies-regiment-in-the-first-world-war.

Lieffers, Caroline. 2018. "How the Panama Canal Took a Huge Toll On the Contract Workers Who Built It." *Smithsonian Magazine*, April 18.

Morgan, Kenneth. 2012. "British Colonial Apprenticeship: Slavery by another name?" *US Slave Blogspot*. January 5. http://usslave.blogspot.com/2012/01/british-colonial-apprenticeship-slavery.html.

Museums, Libraries and Archives Council East of England. 2009. "Case Study 4: Jamaica (1831) - The Rebellion." *The Abolition Project*. http://abolition.e2bn.org/resistance_54.html.

Newton, Velma. 2004. The Silver Men: West Indian Labour Migration to Panama, 1850-1914. Ian Randle Publishers.

Palmer, Ransford W. 2012. Beyond the Horizon: A Jamaican immigrant chases his dream in America. Xlibris Corporation.

Paz B., Sadith Esther. 2014. "The status of West Indian immigrants in Panama." Masters Thesis, Amherst.

Powers, Anne M. 2018. "The Iniquities of Apprenticeship." *A Parcel of Ribbons: Eighteenth century Jamaica viewed through family stories and documents*. February 14. http://aparcelofribbons.co.uk/.

Satchell, Veront. 1999. "Jamaica." *World History Archives*. http://www.hartford-hwp.com/archives/43/130.html.

Small, Sashana. 2019. "You are not the father - DNA tests reveal 70 per cent 'jackets'." *The Jamaica Star*, April 18.

Stephens, Gervanna. 2012. "The Process of Freedom in Jamaica — Apprenticeship being the last stage of slavery than the first stage of freedom." *Academia.* March 29. https://www.academia.edu/7284448/The_Process_of_Freedom_in_Jamaica_Apprenticeship_being_the_last_stage_of_slavery_than_the_first_stage_of_freedom.

The Government of the Republic of Mauritius Aapravasi Ghat Trust Fund. 2006. "An Overview of History of Indenture." *Aapravasi Ghat World Heritage Site.* August 7. http://www.aapravasighat.org/English/Resources%20Research/Documents/History%20of%20Indenture.pdf.

Turner, Mary. 1982. Slaves and Missionaries : The Disintegration of Jamaican Slave Society, 1787–1834. Illinois: University of Illinois Press.

Williams, Paul H. 2014. "Rural Express - Blenheim, Busta's Birthplace Beckons." *The Jamaica Gleaner*, November 15.

APPENDIX I – Cousins, Explained

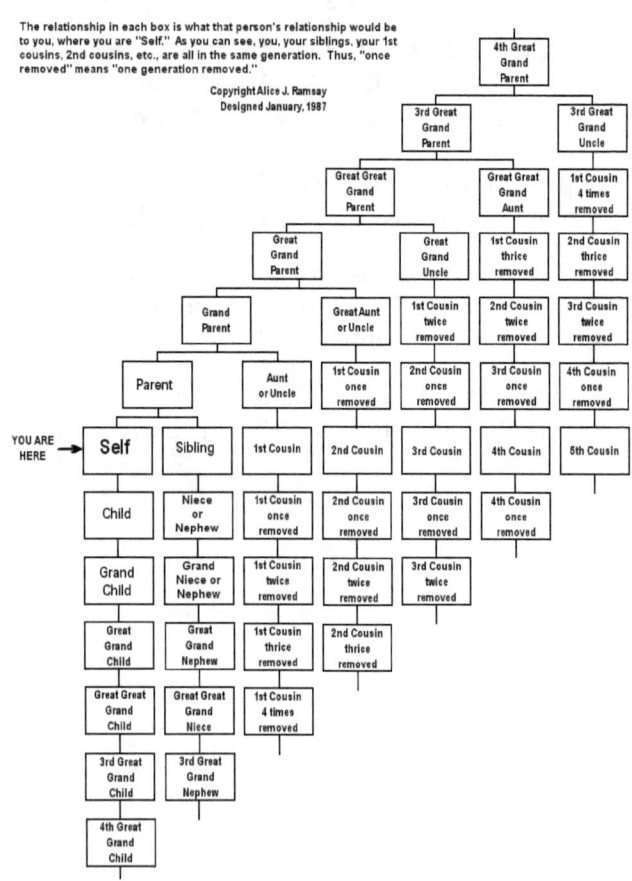

APPENDIX II – My Family Trees

Ambursley & Fairclough

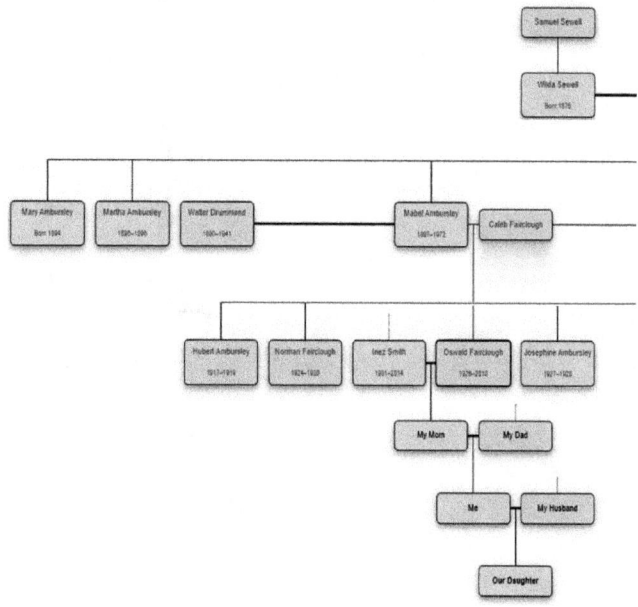

Family Tree

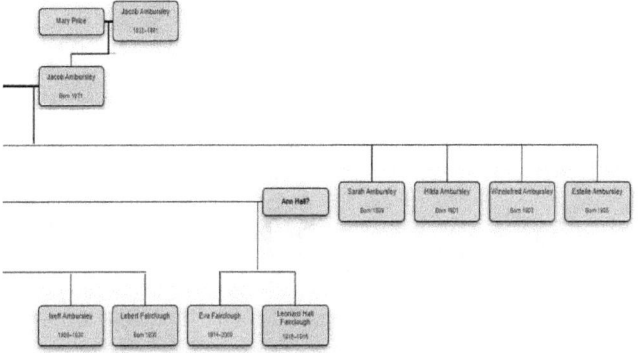

Anglin, Boothe &

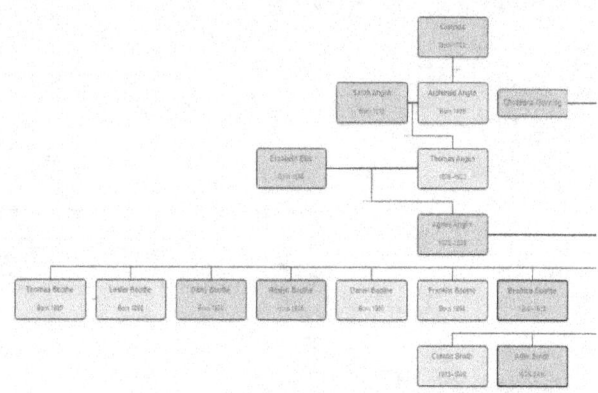

Smith Family Tree

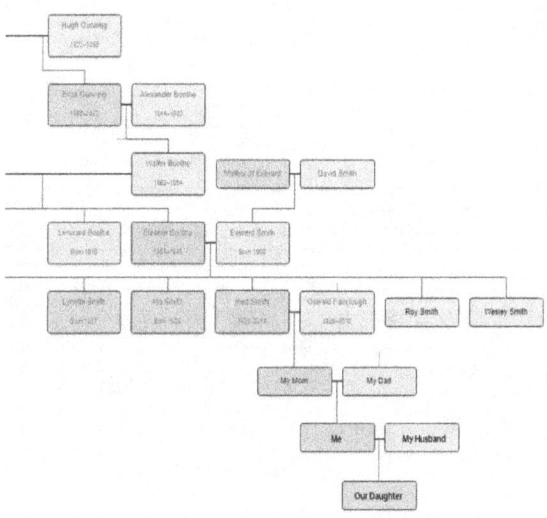

Buckley, Gilzean & Saddler

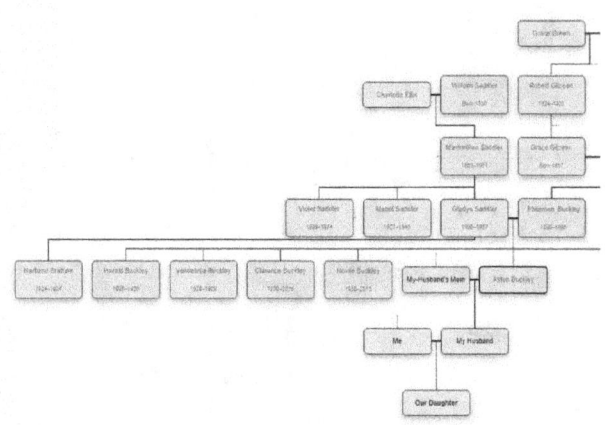

Family Tree

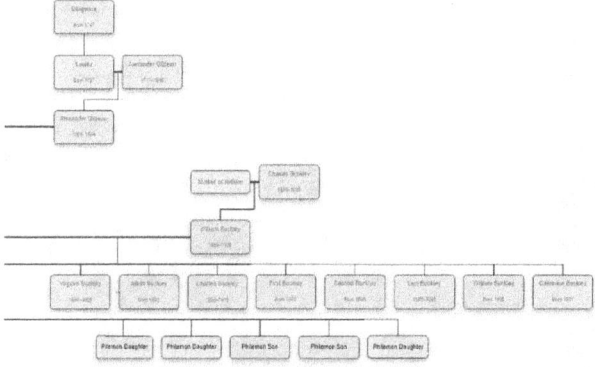

Clarke & Greenfield

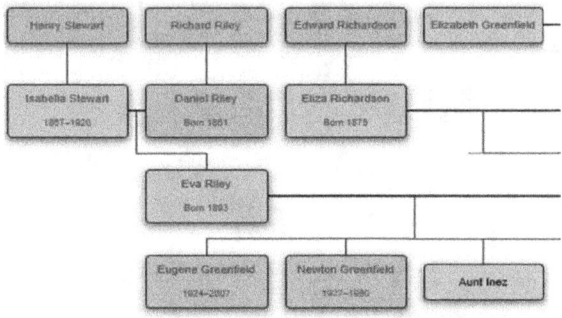

Family Tree

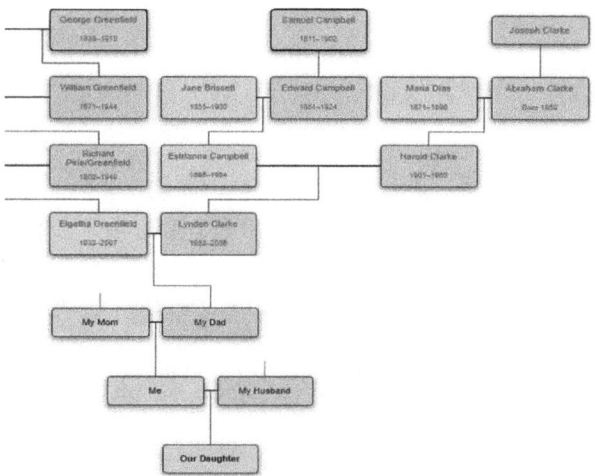

Spencer & Wilson

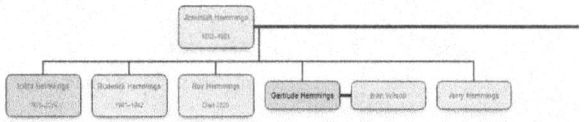

Family Tree

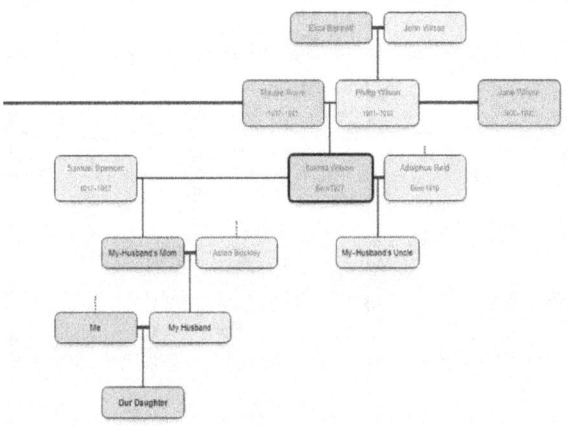

APPENDIX III – RESOURCES CHEAT SHEET

Website	Type	Free?
aparcelofribbons.co.uk	Documented Jamaican family stories and documents	Yes
cyndislist.com	Comprehensive list of online genealogical resources	Yes
earth.google.com	Interactive 3D Earth satellite map	Yes
familyecho.com	Family tree-building software	Yes
familysearch.org	Comprehensive records & family history database	Yes
findagrave.com	Individual burial places (with pictures)	Yes
gedmatch.com	DNA and genealogy tools for comparison and research purposes	Yes
jamaicanfamilysearch.com	Jamaican Genealogy Research Library	Yes

Website	Type	Free?
Legacies of British Slave Ownership ucl.ac.uk/lbs/	Database of British Enslavers in the Caribbean	Yes
obitsjamaica.com	Jamaican Online Obituaries	Yes
ancestry.com	DNA, Genealogy & Records database	Some features
billiongraves.com	Individual burial places (with pictures)	Some features
geni.com	DNA, Genealogy & Records database	Some features
myheritage.com	DNA, Genealogy & Records database	Some features
nationalarchives.gov.uk	British Government Archives	Some features
23andme.com	DNA testing resource	No
findmypast.com	DNA, Genealogy & Records database	No
genealogicalstudies.com	Educational	No
newspaperarchive.com	Worldwide newspaper database	No

Website	Type	Free?
rgd.gov.jm	Registrar General's Department of Jamaica	No

A WORD FROM THE AUTHOR

I hope I have kindled some desire to go beyond the ink and paper of whatever research you are conducting. No matter what your motivation is, it is my wish that you think about the lives symbolized by each document, picture and story you encounter along your journey. I'd love to hear all about the relatives you found, old and new! Share your challenges and triumphs with me on Twitter @ClaudiaCeebee.

www.ingramcontent.com/pod-product-compliance
Lightning Source LLC
LaVergne TN
LVHW051602070426
835507LV00021B/2725